Communications in Computer and Information Science 911

Commenced Publication in 2007
Founding and Former Series Editors:
Phoebe Chen, Alfredo Cuzzocrea, Xiaoyong Du, Orhun Kara, Ting Liu,
Dominik Ślęzak, and Xiaokang Yang

More information about this series at http://www.springer.com/series/7899

Rui Ren · Chen Zheng
Jianfeng Zhan (Eds.)

Big Scientific Data Benchmarks, Architecture, and Systems

First Workshop, SDBA 2018
Beijing, China, June 12, 2018
Revised Selected Papers

 Springer

Editors
Rui Ren
Institute of Computing Technology
Chinese Academy of Sciences
Beijing, China

Jianfeng Zhan
Institute of Computing Technology
Chinese Academy of Sciences
Beijing, China

Chen Zheng
Institute of Computing Technology
Chinese Academy of Sciences
Beijing, China

ISSN 1865-0929   ISSN 1865-0937 (electronic)
Communications in Computer and Information Science
ISBN 978-981-13-5909-5   ISBN 978-981-13-5910-1   (eBook)
https://doi.org/10.1007/978-981-13-5910-1

Library of Congress Control Number: 2018966509

This Springer imprint is published by the registered company Springer Nature Singapore Pte Ltd.
The registered company address is: 152 Beach Road, #21-01/04 Gateway East, Singapore 189721, Singapore

Big Scientific Data: A Rich and Fertile Land

The past several decades witnessed that many scientific projects are data-driven. For example, Aronova et al. [1] discussed the historical connections between two large-scale scientific projects about 50 or 60 years ago that became exemplars for worldwide data-driven scientific initiatives after World War II: the International Geophysical Year (1957–1958; in short, IGY) and the International Biological Program (1964–1974). They concluded [1] that one of the important features of the IGY was its data-driven mode of research, as contrasted with the hypothesis- [3, 4] or instrument-driven mode [5] of most physicists' work and with the platform-driven [6] character of much of the space program.

In recent years, this trend has accelerated, and big scientific data have become the foundation and strategic resources for science discovery and technology innovation. There is increasing interest to generate value from big scientific data. However, efficient management and analysis of big scientific data comprise the first step toward scientific discovery. Scientific data in different domains have unique data schemas, i.e., event data in high-energy physics, RDF data in microbiology, and spatial-temporal data in astronomy. In this context, widely used data management and analytic systems are not necessarily the best choices. The unique characteristics of big scientific data provide new research opportunities. To achieve higher efficiency, we need to tailor both software and hardware architecture to the characteristics of a domain of applications [6, 7]. However, the first step is to fully understand big scientific data.

Without comprehensive big scientific data benchmarks, it is very difficult for scientific researchers and computer system researchers to design and implement high-performance and energy-efficient data management and analytics systems. The NAS parallel benchmarks [8] provide a good example for understanding scientific workloads in terms that the common requirements are specified only algorithmically in a paper-and-pencil approach [8] and are reasonably divorced from individual implementations [9].

In recent years there has been progress in our understanding and modeling of modern big data and AI workloads. Gao et al. [7] consider each big data and AI workload as a pipeline of one or more classes of units of computation performed on different initial or intermediate data inputs, each class of which is called a data motif. They [7] also identify eight data motifs taking up most of the runtime of a wide variety of big data and AI workloads, including Matrix, Sampling, Transform, Graph, Logic, Set, Sort and Statistic computation. Furthermore, they found [7] that significantly different from the traditional kernels [8, 9], a data motif's behaviors are affected by the sizes, patterns, types, and sources of different data inputs. Finally, they [9, 10] propose using the combination of one or more data motifs, to represent diversity of big data and AI workloads, and release a unified big data and AI benchmark suite—BigDataBench 4.0 [9, 10]. This unified benchmark suite sheds new light on domain-specific hardware and software co-design in terms of tailoring the system and architecture to the characteristics of the unified eight data motifs other than one or more applications case by case [7, 9, 10]. However, there is still a long way ahead for big scientific data-specific hardware and software system co-design as there are huge recognition gaps between scientific researchers and computer system researchers. Fortunatelsy, pioneer researchers have paved a path. For example, SciDB [11] is a good attempt of data management system intended primarily for use in application domains that involve very large (petabyte)- scale array data.

Following the past success of BPOE (Big Data benchmarks, Performance Optimization, and Emerging Hardware) workshops [12, 13], we organized the first workshop on Big Scientific Data Benchmarks, Architecture, and Systems (SDBAA 2018; http://prof.ict.ac.cn/sdba18/), which was co-located with ICS 2018 (http://prof.ict.ac.cn/sdba18/)— an ACM International Conference on Supercomputing. The workshop seeks papers that address hot topics in benchmarking, designing, implementing and optimizing big scientific data architecture and systems. This book includes ten papers from the SDBA 2018 workshop.

The call for papers for the workshop attracted a number of high-quality submissions. During a rigorous review process, in which each paper was reviewed by at least three experts, we select ten papers for presentation as SDBA 2018. In addition, we also invited a keynote speaker, Prof. Ziming Zou from the Chinese Academy of Sciences, whose topic was "Big Data Processing and Application Use Cases from China Space Science Missions."

We are very grateful for the efforts of all authors related to writing, revising, and presenting their papers at the SDBA workshop. Finally, we appreciate the indispensable support of the SDBA Program Committee and thank them for their efforts and contributions in maintaining the high standards of the SDBA workshop.

December 2018

Rui Ren
Chen Zheng
Jianfeng Zhan

References

1. E. Aronova, K. S. Baker, and N. Oreskes, Big science and big data in biology: From the international geophysical year through the international biological program to the long term ecological research (lter) network, 1957—present, Hist Stud Nat Sci, vol. 40, no. 2, pp. 183–224, 2010.
2. D. B. Kell and S. G. Oliver, Here is the evidence, now what is the hypothesis? the complementary roles of inductive and hypothesis-driven science in the post-genomic era, Bioessays, vol. 26, no. 1, pp. 99–105, 2004.
3. U. Krohs and W. Callebaut, Data without models merging with models without data, in Systems biology. Elsevier, 2007, pp. 181–213.
4. P. Galison, Image and logic: A material culture of microphysics. University of Chicago Press, 1997.

5. D. H. DeVorkin, Science with a vengeance: how the military created the us space sciences after world war ii, Science With A Vengeance. How the Military Created the US Space Sciences After World War II, XXII, 404 pp. 109 figs. Springer-Verlag Berlin Heidelberg New York. Also Springer Study Edition, p. 109, 1992.

6. J. Hennessy and D. Patterson, A new golden age for computer architecture: Domain-specific hardware/software co-design, enhanced security, open instruction sets, and agile chip development, 2018.

7. W. Gao, J. Zhan, L. Wang, C. Luo, D. Zheng, F. Tang, B. Xie, C. Zheng, X. Wen, X. He, H. Ye, and R. Ren, Data motifs: A lens towards fully understanding big data and ai workloads, Parallel Architectures and Compilation Techniques (PACT), 27th International Conference on, 2018.

8. D. H. Bailey, E. Barszcz, J. T. Barton, D. S. Browning, R. L. Carter, L. Dagum, R. A. Fatoohi, P. O. Frederickson, T. A. Lasinski, R. S. Schreiber et al., The nas parallel benchmarks, The International Journal of Supercomputing Applications, vol. 5, no. 3, pp. 63–73, 1991.

9. K. Asanovic, R. Bodik, B. C. Catanzaro, J. J. Gebis, P. Husbands, K. Keutzer, D. A. Patterson,W. L. Plishker, J. Shalf, S.W. Williams, and Y. Katherine, The landscape of parallel computing research: A view from berkeley, Technical Report UCB/EECS-2006-183, EECS Department, University of California, Berkeley, Tech. Rep., 2006.

10. W. Gao, J. Zhan, L. Wang, C. Luo, D. Zheng, X. Wen, R. Ren, C. Zheng, H. Ye, J. Dai, Z. Cao, et al., Bigdatabench: A scalable and unified big data and ai benchmark suite, Under review of IEEE Transaction on Parallel and Distributed Systems, 2018.

11. L. Wang, J. Zhan, C. Luo, Y. Zhu, Q. Yang, Y. He, W. Gao, Z. Jia, Y. Shi, S. Zhang et al., Bigdatabench: A big data benchmark suite from internet services, IEEE International Symposium On High Performance Computer Architecture (HPCA), 2014.

12. Stonebraker, M., Brown, P., Zhang, D., & Becla, J. (2013). SciDB: A database management system for applications with complex analytics. Computing in Science & Engineering, 15(3), 54-62.

13. J. Zhan, R. Han, C. Weng. Big Data Benchmarks, Performance Optimization, and Emerging Hardware, Springer LNCS, volume 8807, 2014.

14. J. Zhan, R. Han, R. V. Zicari. Big Data Benchmarks, Performance Optimization, and Emerging Hardware, Springer LNCS, volume 9495, 2016.

Organization

Program Co-chairs

Rui Ren   Institute of Computing Technology, Chinese Academy
of Sciences and University of Chinese Academy
of Sciences, China

Xiaoyong Du   Renmin University of China, China

Jianfeng Zhan   Institute of Computing Technology, Chinese Academy
of Sciences and University of Chinese Academy
of Sciences, China

General Chairs

Chen Zheng   Institute of Computing Technology, Chinese Academy
of Sciences and University of Chinese Academy
of Sciences, China

Jianhui Li   Computer Network Information Center, Chinese Academy
of Sciences, China

Program Committee

Xiaoyi Lu   The Ohio State University, USA

Hyogi Sim   Oak Ridge National Laboratory, USA

Gwangsun Kim   ARM Ltd.

Nikhil Jain   Lawrence Livermore National Laboratory, USA

Weijia Xu   The University of Texas at Austin, USA

Zhihui Du   Tsinghua University, China

Lei Wang   Institute of Computing Technology, Chinese Academy
of Sciences, China

Shengzhong Feng   Shenzhen Institutes of Advanced Technology, Chinese
Academy of Sciences, China

Jiaquan Gao   Nanjing Normal University, China

Hua Zhong   Institute of Software, Chinese Academy of Sciences, China

Li Zha   Institute of Computing Technology, Chinese Academy
of Sciences, China

Yunquan Zhang   Institute of Computing Technology, Chinese Academy
of Sciences, China

Cheqing Jin   East China Normal University, China

Yuanming Zhang   Zhejiang University of Technology, China

Wenyao Zhang   Beijing Institute of Technology, China

Xiaoru Yuan   Peking University, China

Contents

Benchmarking

GCM-Bench: A Benchmark for RDF Data Management System on Microorganism Data

Renfeng Liu$^{(\boxtimes)}$ and Jungang Xu

University of Chinese Academy of Sciences, Beijing, China
liurenfeng16@mails.ucas.ac.cn, xujg@ucas.ac.cn

Abstract. The biological data is growing up to an unprecedented scale, such as microorganism knowledge graph organized by biologists, which is represented by Resource Description Framework (RDF) data model. In this paper, GCM-Bench, a new benchmark to evaluate the performance of general-purpose RDF data management systems on microorganism RDF data is proposed, which consists of microorganism RDF data generator, SPARQL query workloads and automatic test system, that can execute the testing workloads automatically and monitor the resource utilization. Five RDF data management systems are selected for evaluation on different sizes of data using automatic test system. We think GCM-Bench will help microbiologists and system developers to select their proper RDF data management system.

Keywords: Benchmark · RDF · SPARQL · Scientific computing Evaluation · Microorganism

1 Introduction

Resource Description Framework (RDF), proposed by W3C, is originally defined as a standard for representing meta data about Web resources. Meanwhile, it is also a popular data model for describing, merging and releasing public datasets. RDF is a very flexible graph-like data model and thus it can be used to merge datasets with different schemas and kinds. It is also widely used in knowledge management like Google Knowledge Graph.

The biological data is growing up to an unprecedented scale, including data produced by modern scientific instruments and data organized by biologists. However, there is not a tool or system is developed specifically for the data organized by biologist. Now we need to manage a big microorganism data containing 10 billion RDF triples. It is difficult to deal with these huge and complex data in general-purpose systems.

Various RDF data management systems have been built based on different approaches with the considerable attention of RDF more and more. However, these systems cannot deliver good performance uniformly across diverse datasets

© Springer Nature Singapore Pte Ltd. 2019
R. Ren et al. (Eds.): SDBA 2018, CCIS 911, pp. 3–14, 2019.
https://doi.org/10.1007/978-981-13-5910-1_1

and varied workloads. So, it is necessary to develop a benchmark for evaluating RDF data management systems. In this paper, GCM-Bench, a benchmark for evaluating the performance of general-purpose RDF data management systems on microorganism is proposed, which is used to compare the widely used RDF data management systems in biological field.

The contribution of this paper are as follows:

- A new benchmark called GCM-Bench is developed for specific biological field, which contains data generator, SPARQL query workloads and automatic test system. However, automatic test system is a general-purpose benchmark executing system separated from data generator and SPARQL query workloads. It can execute a benchmark on RDF data management systems regardless of the architecture of them, and it can also generate a report.
- Several widely used general-purpose RDF data management systems with different sizes of data and workloads are evaluated with GCM-Bench, and from the experimental results, we summarize the performance of the systems on microorganism knowledge graph are analyzed and some suggestions are given.

The rest of this paper is organized as follows. In the next Section (Sect. 2) we briefly introduce the basic knowledge of RDF and SPARQL. Section 3 discusses the related RDF data management systems and benchmarks. We introduce GCM-Bench in detail in Sect. 4 and present the experimental results comparing the performance of related systems on microorganism RDF data in Sect. 5. Finally, we analyze the reasons for the performance of these systems and give the conclusions in Sect. 6.

2   RDF and SPARQL

RDF is a semantic Web data model and represents data as a collection of triples. A triple consists of three parts, in the form of (subject, predicate, object), or $t = (s, p, o)$. Both the subject and object are entities or classes of resources, and object can be also a literal value. Predicate denotes attributes of the resources or relationship between the subject and the object. A triple can be interpreted as 'the value of property p of s is o' or 's is connected with o by relation p'. So, a set of triples can be represented as a directed labeled Graph $G = \{t_1, t_2, ...t_n\}$. Figure 1(b) visualizes RDF graph of RDF triple set in Fig. 1(a).

SPARQL (a recursive acronym for SPARQL Protocol and RDF Query Language) is the standard query language recommend by W3C for RDF and provides a series of methods or protocols to query and manipulate RDF data. A basic SPARQL query is usually composed of two parts: the query conditions and the query output. The query conditions contain a set of triples, which differ from RDF triples in that any of the subject, predicate and object may be a variable. The following SPARQL query is an example that means to retrieve the name of person who has a email address bob@example.com.

subject	predicate	object
Abraham_Lincoln	title	president
Abraham_Lincoln	bornIn	Hodgenvillel_KY
Abraham_Lincoln	diedIn	Washington_DC
Washington_DC	foundingYear	1790
United_States	hasCapital	Washington_DC
Hodgenvillel_KY	locatedIn	United_States

(a) RDF triples

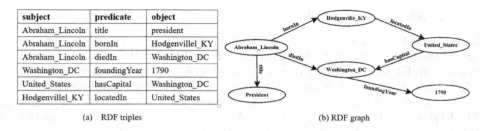

(b) RDF graph

Fig. 1. An example of RDF graph

```
SELECT ?name WHERE {
    ?person name ?name.
    ?person email 'bob@example.com'.
}
```

3 Related Work

3.1 Microorganism Knowledge Graph

Microorganism knowledge graph is an enormous RDF database in microbiology fields, which covers most information about microorganism including taxonomy, protein, enzyme, gene and so on. Biological scientists can query information they want from microorganism knowledge graph, rather than collecting it from different data sources.

3.2 RDF Data Management Systems

Many RDF data management systems are proposed during the past decades. Jena [1], Sesame [2] (known as rdf4j now) are early RDF data management systems and they are still popular now. RDF-3X [3] created its own storage implementation and supports compressed indexes. Hexastore [6] proposed a sextuple-indexing schema for quick and scalabel general-purpose query processing. SW-Store [7] uses vertical partitioning and column-oriented DBMS to achieve high performance RDF data management. gStore [8] stores RDF data and represents SPARQL query in the form of graph, and thus processes SPARQL query by subgraph matching.

In order to break the limitations of single machine, many parallel and distributed systems emerged. S2RDF [4] stores RDF data on Hadoop and executes SPARQL using Spark [11]. gStoreD [8,9] uses some graph partitioning algorithm such as METIS [14] to partition RDF graph into vertex-disjoint fragments and stores fragments on different nodes. However, full SPARQL query need to execute on each node to find local partial matches and the final result is the crossing matches of partial result.

3.3   SPARQL Benchmarks

In the recent decades, many benchmarks for SPARQL query processing systems have arisen. Lehigh University Benchmark (LUBM) [15] is a widely used benchmark for comparing the reasoning capabilities and storage mechanisms of OWL reasoning engines. It uses universities and departments ontology to evaluate semantic inferencing, but it is not suitable for the systems intended for SPARQL query. DBpedia SPARQL Benchmark measures the number of queries the system can answer in one second on DBpedia knowledge base. But the size of dataset is fixed and can't be scaled, which limits the test on parallel and distributed systems. SP^{2}Bench [17] is a SPARQL performance benchmark settled in DBLP scenario. However, the performance maybe not be accurate in another specific scenoario. The experiments of Aluç et al. [18] show that existing RDF data management systems cannot provide good performance consistent across workloads and datasets. Besides, there are a lot of benchmarks for big data like BigDataBench [22,23], Data Motifs [24,25]. In order to find out a suitable system for microbiology knowledge graph, a specific benchmark is essential and critical.

4   GCM-Bench

GCM-Bench is an integrated benchmark environment for RDF data management system, which is composed of data generator, SPARQL query workloads and automatic test system. It is aimed at evaluating the performance of RDF data management systems on microorganism data. The automatic test system uses simulated data generated by data generator and workloads to perform benchmark tests on the selected systems. Source code can be accessed in https://github.com/renfliu/gcm-bench.

4.1   Data Generator

Global microorganism knowledge graph is published by The Institute of Microbiology, Chinese Academy of Sciences. It aims at changing the current status of heterogeneity, alienation, and poor association of microorganism data, and provides query systems for global microbial researchers through integrating multiple datasets with different types. The microorganism dataset contains enzyme data, protein data, gene data, et al. The microorganism dataset is stored in Notation3 [21], one shorthand non-XML serialization of RDF. Part of the structure of mocroorganism data is shown in Fig. 2.

The size of origin dataset is limited, so it is necessary to design a data generator to meet evaluation needs. We performed statistical analysis on the existing datasets and obtained the corresponding proportions and location information of each component in the dataset. Based on the statistical information of data, we designed a simulated data generator, which can produce a specific number of RDF triples by parameters. The number of instances of each class has a great influence on the generative rules of the ID that is used to establish the connection between instances.

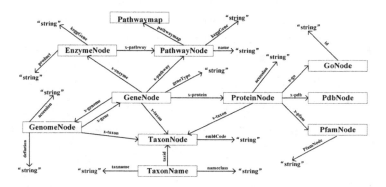

Fig. 2. Microorganism RDF data structure

There may be more than one object in the triple with same property and subject. By analyzing the existing data, we simulated the distribution of the number of objects and created a distribution function for each of it, since uniform distribution can be used to transform any distribution with inverse function. For example, the number function of genes in genome is like $Num = Max - N * (\log_e R \div \log_e c)$. The Max is the maximum of the generated objects. The c can control the speed of change in quantity and N is the amplification coefficient, expanding the random number to fit the quantity range. R is a random number generated by uniform distribution. A suitable number function for gene comes into being by adjusting the parameters.

The data generator can produce up to terabytes of data. In addition to specifying the number of triples, the tool also provides parameters for class proportion setting to customize the data according to different needs.

4.2 Workloads

SPARQL is the standard RDF data access approach for RDF data management systems, and it reflects the data processing performance of management systems. When selecting the query workloads, we follow two principles: (1) Design the queries according to the specific features of SPARQL language. (2) Base on the specific requirements for microbiological researchers. Finally, we select 16 query statements as our basic workloads and provide 4 update statements as additional workloads.

According to the structural features of SPARQL query proposed by Aluç et al., we analyzed the workloads and the results are shown in Fig. 3. The first four queries focus on basic select statement of SPARQL and no other features. Constraint functions in where clause are evaluated in queries 2, 3, 4, and algebra functions and result modifiers (such *ORDER BY*) are in Query 5 to Query 9. The last four queries are combined queries based on statements that the biologists actually use.

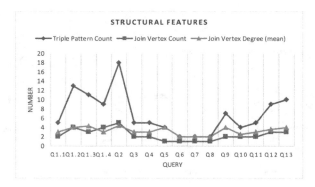

Fig. 3. Structural features of SPARQL query

4.3 Automatic Test System

In order to be more precise and convenient in evaluating the existing RDF data management systems, we built an automatic test system for GCM-Bench, which integrates a series of tools for testing, including data generator, workloads, system monitoring tools, report generator, and test task scheduler. This is a general-purpose testing framework that supports most RDF data management systems. The only thing you need to do is to write a driver program to connect the RDF system with the framework and then the testing tasks will run automatically and an evaluation report will be generated as a result. Another feature of the framework is that you can customize datasets and workloads in the configuration file.

Firstly, the data generator will generate a specific size of data file stored on the local disk and the data file will be imported into RDF data management system through the interface in the driver. Then the test tasks will be executed in turn according to the workloads arrangement. Meanwhile, the monitoring tools will collect the whole system's and the management system's resource utilization. After all, the system writes the results of the SPARQL workloads and resources utilization to an HTML report, which shows the results in an intuitive way for researchers.

5 Experiment and Evaluation

To find the RDF data management systems with good performance on microorganism RDF data, we use GCM-Bench to evaluate several widely used RDF data management systems. We follow three principles to select the systems for benchmark: (1) the popularity of the system, (2) the degree of innovativeness, (3) whether it is continuously updated. Finally, the selected RDF data management systems are RDF-3X, gStore(v0.5), Virtuoso(VOS v7.2.4.2), 4Store(v1.1.6), and Jena(v3.7).

5.1   Experiment Setup

Standalone experiments are running on a high performance rack server with two E5-2640v4 processors, containing 40 cores totally, 128 GB memory and 8TB disk space. The storage is configured in RAID 5 with eight 1TB disks. There are two kinds of data we use, one is real dataset, another is simulated dataset. The details of dataset are shown in Table 1. We used GH-RDF3X for RDF-3X and selected TDB2 of Jena as Jena's database.

Table 1. The details of dataset

Dataset	Triple number	Data size
real data	286,000,000	46 GB
gcm1m	1,000,000	141 MB
gcm10m	10,000,000	1.4 GB
gcm100m	100,000,000	14 GB
gcm500m	500,000,000	70 GB
gcm1b	1,000,000,000	139 GB

The experiments can be divided into two parts: the data loading experiments and the SPARQL query experiments. In data loading experiments, the original triple data will be imported into the RDF data management system and stored in a new schema. The SPARQL query experiments can be classifies into several categories:

- **Cold queries and warm-up queries:** In order to speed up the query process, some systems adopt a cache approach to store frequently accessed data in memory. To eliminate this effect, we divide queries into cold queries and warm-up queries. Warm-up queries are based on caching and learning strategies of the systems, while cold queries are not. When performing a cold query, we need to restart the system every time to clear the cache in the system.
- **Concurrent queries:** The concurrent processing capability of the system is also an important performance indicator. We performed measurement runs with 2, 4, 8, 16 and 64 clients concurrently.
- **Update statements:** Most RDF data management systems support query statements of SPARQL language, but update statements are supported limited. For the systems that support update statements, we provide several update workloads to test them.

5.2   Performance Metrics

To demonstrate the difference of the performance, we select some metrics for the benchmark, including load time, repository size, query response time. They are also standard database benchmark metrics. While workloads are running, the monitoring tool can collect the resource utilization for calculating the metrics.

- **Load Time:** During loading process, the RDF data management systems will perform a series of pre-processing tasks, such as creating indexes for RDF data, converting triples into relational models or graph models, replacing strings with ids, and so on.
- **Repository Size:** After loading process, the disk space occupied by the repository is a matter of concern, because people always make a tradeoff between time and space.
- **Query Response Time:** Query response time is one of the most important metrics for a database. It refers to the time spent from submitting a query statement to getting results.

In each query, some literal values are given by parameters, which are usually generated by rules. We use the same values in different systems for comparative experiments to obtain the same result to verify correctness. But in a concurrent query experiment, we used random seeds to generate different values in 100 queries.

5.3   Experimental Results and Analysis

Load Time. Table 2 shows the speed of loading data on each system and the size of the repository on a single machine. In general, as the size of data set grows, the load time of each system also increases linearly. For 100 million or less triple data set, except for Jena, all other systems have roughly equal load time. Virtuoso is the fastest one in small data sets, but as the amount of data increases, so dose the time spent, even for the dataset with more than 100 million triples. During the loading process, 4Store loads all the data into memory regardless of the memory limit, so it often failed on big dataset. Both RDF3X and gStore perform well, they have similar and stable performance in this process whether the dataset is large or small. Considering the size of repository, RDF3X is the smallest, about half of the original data, thanks to its unique compression technology. Other system repositories are basically the same size, only slightly larger than the original data.

Not all systems perform well on large data sets. Virtuoso dose not respond after 3 days of loading 500 million triple data. When 4store loads 100 million and more triple data, the loading process is assumed to be normal and a successful result is returned, but the actual repository is only tens of KB. RDF3X, gStore and Jena all have good performance when processing large amounts of data on a single machine.

Cold Queries. Figure 4 shows the cold query response time (in milliseconds) of the systems. The blank place means that the system does not support the SPARQL feature of the query. We can see that gStore, RDF3X, Virtuoso and 4Store perform similarly and Jena's response time is always a bit more than others. But Jena has the most complete support for SPARQL language and stable performance regardless of the size of data. RDF3X has the shortest response

Table 2. Load time on single machine

Systems	1 M	10 M	100 M	500 M
gStore	12.617 s/197 MB	119.878 s/1.8 GB	1307.257 s/16 GB	9269.568 s/72 GB
RDF3X	8.890 s/96 MB	110.299 s/893 MB	1345.489 s/8.2 GB	7632.564 s/43 GB
Jena	30.515 s/181 MB	233.597 s/1.8 GB	2859.633 s/16 GB	60320.939 s/77 GB
4store	10.509 s/187 MB	103.298 s/1.3 GB	Failed	Failed
Virtuoso 7	5.319 s	100.460 s	11420.026 s	Failed

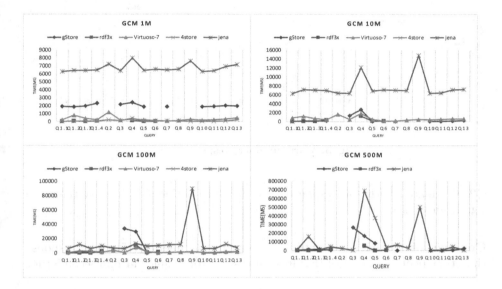

Fig. 4. Cold query response time

time, but only supports basic select queries and cannot be applied to actual use. Virtuoso and 4Store both have problems on large datasets. gStore is not the best one on response time, stability and complete support on SPARQL, but it performs well and has no letdown.

Warm-up Queries. The query processing method of Jena TDB's is the same as gStore. The database information, like index structure, needs to be loaded to memory as soon as the system starts. After that, the system start to process the query. Virtuoso supports caching technology, which can cache frequently-queried data and last-query data in memory. When a new query arrives, Virtuoso can use cache and indexes in memory to speed up query processing. Figure 5 shows the warm-up query response time (in milliseconds) of these three systems. We can see that the response time of these systems are similar and they all have ups and downs. On Q4, Virtuoso is always the best one but it is opposite on

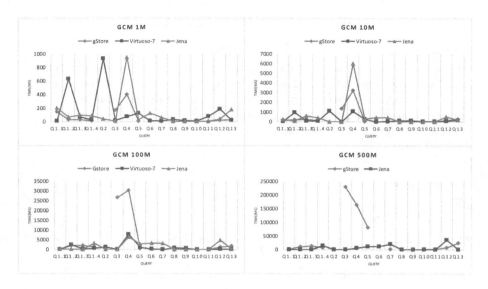

Fig. 5. Warm-up query response time

Q2. Compared with the response time of cold queries, all three systems are significantly fast.

Concurrent Queries. In actual use, concurrent queries affect the response time that people really feel. Figure 6 shows the total time (in milliseconds) for

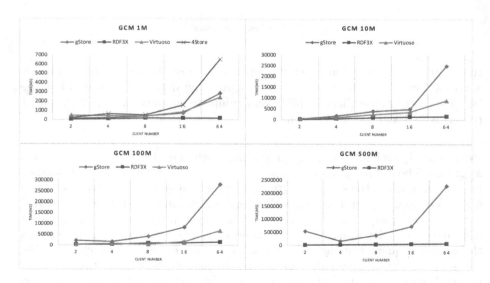

Fig. 6. Concurrent query response time

all queries when multiple clients simultaneously query each system. RDF3X is the fastest one, because it starts multiple independent processes to process each query, while other systems share the same resources to handle concurrency. gStore does not support concurrency and can only execute each query sequentially, so it is the slowest one. Virtuoso is in the middle, but there are some problems with large datasets for it.

6 Conclusions

A RDF data management system performance evaluation benchmark for microorganism knowledge graph called GCM-Bench is proposed in this paper. Each RDF data management systems has its own use of the scene. The comparative experiments show the advantages and disadvantages of each system, and we hope it will help microbiologists and system developers to select their proper systems.

Acknowledgment. This work is supported by the National Key Research and Development Plan of China (Grant No. 2016YFB1000600 and 2016YFB1000601).

References

1. Carroll, J. J., Dickinson, I., Dollin, C., Reynolds, D., Seaborne, A., Wilkinson, K.: Jena: implementing the semantic web recommendations. In: Proceedings of the 13th International World Wide Web Conference - Alternate Track Papers & Posters, pp. 74–83. ACM, New York (2004)
2. Broekstra, J., Kampman, A., van Harmelen, F.: Sesame: a generic architecture for storing and querying RDF and RDF schema. In: Horrocks, I., Hendler, J. (eds.) ISWC 2002. LNCS, vol. 2342, pp. 54–68. Springer, Heidelberg (2002). https://doi.org/10.1007/3-540-48005-6_7
3. Neumann, T., Weikum, G.: RDF-3X: a RISC-style engine for RDF. Proc. VLDB Endow. **1**(1), 647–659 (2008)
4. Schätzle, A., Przyjaciel-Zablocki, M., Skilevic, S., Lausen, G.: S2RDF: RDF querying with SPARQL on spark. Proc. VLDB Endow. **9**(10), 804–815 (2016)
5. Peng, P., Zou, L., Özsu, M.T., Chen, L., Zhao, D.: Processing SPARQL queries over distributed RDF graphs. VLDB J. **25**(2), 243–268 (2016)
6. Weiss, C., Karras, P., Bernstein, A.: Hexastore: sextuple indexing for semantic web data management. Proc. VLDB Endow. **1**(1), 1008–1019 (2008)
7. Abadi, D.J., Marcus, A., Madden, S.R., Hollenbach, K.: SW-Store: a vertically partitioned DBMS for semantic web data management. VLDB J. **18**(2), 385–406 (2009)
8. Zou, L., Özsu, M.T., Chen, L., Shen, X., Huang, R., Zhao, D.: gStore: a graph-based SPARQL query engine. VLDB J. **23**(4), 565–590 (2014)
9. Zou, L., Mo, J., Chen, L., Özsu, M.T., Zhao, D.: gStore: answering SPARQL queries via subgraph matching. Proc. VLDB Endow. **4**(8), 482–493 (2011)
10. Özsu, M.T.: A survey of RDF data management systems. Front. Comput. Sci. **10**(3), 418–432 (2016)

11. Zaharia, M., Chowdhury, M., Franklin, M.J., Shenker, S., Stoica, I.: Spark: cluster computing with working sets. In: Proceedings of the 2nd USENIX Workshop on Hot Topics in Cloud Computing, vol. 10, no. 10–10, p. 95. USENIX Association, Boston (2010)
12. Zeng, K., Yang, J., Wang, H., Shao, B., Wang, Z.: A distributed graph engine for web scale RDF data. Proc. VLDB Endow. **6**(4), 265–276 (2013)
13. Shao, B., Wang, H., Li, Y.: Trinity: a distributed graph engine on a memory cloud. In: Proceedings of the 2013 ACM SIGMOD International Conference on Management of Data, pp. 505–516. ACM, New York (2013)
14. Karypis, G., Kumar, V.: Analysis of multilevel graph partitioning. In: Proceedings of the 1995 ACM/IEEE Conference on Supercomputing. ACM, New York (1995)
15. Guo, Y., Pan, Z., Heflin, J.: LUBM: a benchmark for OWL knowledge base systems. Web Semant. Sci. Serv. Agents World Wide Web **3**(2–3), 158–182 (2005)
16. Ma, L., Yang, Y., Qiu, Z., Xie, G., Pan, Y., Liu, S.: Towards a complete OWL ontology benchmark. In: Sure, Y., Domingue, J. (eds.) ESWC 2006. LNCS, vol. 4011, pp. 125–139. Springer, Heidelberg (2006). https://doi.org/10.1007/11762256_12
17. Schmidt, M., Hornung, T., Lausen, G., Pinkel, C.: SP^{2}Bench: a SPARQL performance benchmark. In: Proceedings of the 25th International Conference on Data Engineering, pp. 222–233. IEEE Computer Society, Shanghai, China (2009)
18. Aluç, G., Hartig, O., Özsu, M.T., Daudjee, K.: Diversified stress testing of RDF data management systems. In: Mika, P., et al. (eds.) ISWC 2014. LNCS, vol. 8796, pp. 197–212. Springer, Cham (2014). https://doi.org/10.1007/978-3-319-11964-9_13
19. Bizer, C., Schultz, A.: The Berlin SPARQL benchmark. Int. J. Semant. Web Inf. Syst. **5**(2), 1–24 (2009)
20. Feng, J., Meng, C., Song, J., Zhang, X., Feng, Z., Zou, L.: SPARQL query parallel processing: a survey. In: Proceedings of the 2017 IEEE International Congress on Big Data, pp. 444–451. IEEE Computer Society, Honolulu (2017)
21. Berners-Lee, T., Connolly, D.: Notation3 (N3): a readable RDF syntax. https://www.w3.org/TeamSubmission/n3/. Last Accessed 2 Apr 2018
22. Wang, L., Zhan, J., Luo, C., Zhu, Y., Yang, Q., et al.: Bigdatabench: a big data benchmark suite from internet services. In: IEEE International Symposium On High Performance Computer Architecture (HPCA), pp. 488–499 (2014)
23. Jia, Z., Zhan, J., Wang, L., Luo, C., Gao, W., Jin, Y., et al.: Understanding big data analytics workloads on modern processors. IEEE Trans. Parallel Distrib. Syst. **28**(6), 1797–1810 (2017)
24. Gao, W., Zhan, J., Wang, L., Luo, C., Zheng, D., et al.: Data Motifs: a lens towards fully understanding big data and AI workloads. In: Parallel Architectures and Compilation Techniques (PACT). IEEE, Limassol, Cyprus (2018)
25. Gao, W., Zhan, J., Wang, L., Luo, C., Jia, Z., et al.: Data Motif-based proxy benchmarks for big data and AI workloads. In: 2018 IEEE International Symposium on Workload Characterization. IEEE, Raleigh (2018)

Evaluating Index Systems of High Energy Physics

Shaopeng Dai[1,2(✉)], Wanling Gao[1,2], Biwei Xie[1,2], Minghe Yu[1,2],
Jia'nan Chen[2], Defei Kong[1,2], Rui Han[1], and Jinheng Li[3]

[1] Institute of Computing Technology, Chinese Academy of Sciences, Beijing, China
{daishaopeng,gaowanling,xiebiwei,yuminghe,kongdefei,hanrui}@ict.ac.cn
[2] University of Chinese Academy of Sciences, Beijing, China
chenjianan14@mails.ucas.ac.cn
[3] Sichuan University, Chengdu, China
leeebucks@gmail.com

Abstract. Nowadays, more and more scientific data has been produced through high-energy physics *(HEP)* facilities. Even in one particle physics experiment, the generated data reaches to petabytes scale. Retrieving data from massive data occupies a large proportion of data processing in HEP. Hence, the data query latency and throughput are the most important metrics for HEP data management. Inspired by the indexing technology of databases, the technology that improves the performance of data retrieval through the HEP data indexing, becomes the mainstream in the HEP data management. In this paper, focusing on two typical index systems–MySQL and HBase–for HEP data management, which are the typical SQL and NoSQL system respectively, we evaluate them from the perspectives of overall performance, system and microarchitecture behaviors. We find that HBase achieves higher performance than MySQL with the data scale increasing.

Keywords: High-energy physics · Data management · Event index HBase · MySQL

1 Introduction

In high-energy physics, many large scientific facilities have been built to study significant issues, including Large Hadron Collider (LHC), Beijing Electron-Positron Collider (BEPC) and other devices. More and more data has been generated from various experimental facilities. Nowadays, the overall accumulated data in high-energy physics reaches to 1000PB and still keeps increasing. Physicists around the world now face great challenges on how to efficiently manage and analyze massive data. One large HEP experiment can produce billions or trillions of events. Physicists are only interested in very few events in one physical analysis task. The data retrieval accounts for a large proportion of HEP data processing. And the data query latency and throughput are most important metrics

© Springer Nature Singapore Pte Ltd. 2019
R. Ren et al. (Eds.): SDBA 2018, CCIS 911, pp. 15–26, 2019.
https://doi.org/10.1007/978-981-13-5910-1_2

for HEP data management. Inspired by the indexing technology of databases, the technology [15] that improves the performance of data retrieval through the HEP data indexing becomes the mainstream in the HEP data management.

The features of HEP data, for example, multi-source and heterogeneity, raise great challenges for HEP data management and processing. First, HEP data is generated from different modern scientific facilities in various scenarios. Second, the HEP data is inherently heterogeneous, with different data structures. Third, physicists of HEP, who plan to obtain specific insights, their interests of the collected data are quite different. To facilitate the data management and analytics, many index systems are introduced into HEP experiments. In this paper, we characterize two typical index systems in HEP data management, which are HBase [2] and MySQL [3]. We investigate their query efficiency, system and architectural behaviors.

We further design series of experiments on data sets that gather from real world around us, and the workloads are representative in high-energy physics.

The observations from our experiments are as follows:

- With the expansion of data scale, the HBase's performance is better than MySQL's, in terms of both throughput and latency.
- MySQL suffers from more I/O waits than that of HBase.
- The memory bandwidth of MySQL is very high compared to HBase. In HEP scenarios, the index systems have low bandwidth requirements.
- The IPC of both MySQL and HBase are low, due to the massive frontend and backend stalls. All cache misses of HBase are lower than that of MySQL, except L2 cache miss.
- Compared with Hbase, MySQL has a lower ratio in branch prediction. In HEP scenarios, the index systems have low bandwidth requirements.
- The operation intensity of MySQL is lower than that of HBase, for all three data scale configurations.

Here is this paper's organization: In Sect. 2, we discuss the background curtly. Section 3 discusses experimental design. Section 4 elaborates experimental results and analysis. At last, we present the conclusion in Sect. 5.

2   Background

In this part, there is a description about HEP experiment and elaborate its procedure of data collection and organization. Then, we will introduce two commonly used index systems in HEP data management—HBase and MySQL.

HEP Experiment. High-energy physics, which also called particle physics, is a physics branch to discover the nature of particles. There are four procedures in an HEP experiment [15]: data filtering, data reconstruction, data analysis and simulations. Data in an HEP experiment are generated by the high-speed collisions of particles in the accelerator and captured by the detector. After being filtered by online system, these data are transferred to offline system and stored on disks as raw data, which are organized as events. Event is the basic data unit of HEP and one large HEP experiment can produce trillions of events. Then, the data are reconstructed and saved as ROOT-format files, on which physicists will use the data analysis frameworks (e.g. ROOT [4,5], BEAN) to conduct in-depth analysis.

Event Index System. There are lots of events being collected in an HEP experiment. However, physicists are only interested in a small part of them in one specific physical analysis task. Inspired by the indexing technology of databases, the technology that improves the performance of data retrieval through the HEP data indexing, becomes the mainstream in the HEP data management. Indexes can be created through a database table, which will facilitate rapid lookups and efficient accesses. High-energy physical data processing has a very high concurrent access. Aiming at good scalability and performance, HBase [13] and MySQL [3] are introduced to build the index system in HEP data management. With event index systems, we firstly scan the database using filtering conditions to find the corresponding record, and thus its inverted index. Then we use inverted index to finally get the events which physicists are interested in.

3   Experimental Methodology

This section presents our experiment methodology. As Fig. 1 tells, we first choose real world data sets of high-energy physics. After analyzing the features of HEP data, we select the typical workloads from high-energy physics and build a workload generator to preserve the real workload patterns, including the number of queries and query arriving rate. When the index database receives a user query, it runs and return a list of result to satisfy the query. In addition, we select three categories of metrics to evaluate two typical index systems for HEP data management. The following sections will introduce chosen data sets, workloads, the workload generator, metrics and our experimental setup in detail.

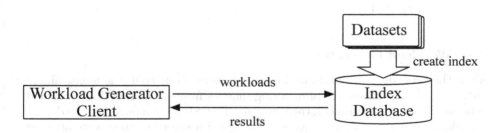

Fig. 1. Experimental methodology.

3.1   Chosen Data Sets

When doing the experiments, three data sets of the BESIII Beijing spectrometer [12] are selected. The three data sets contain 11645 ROOT files (425 million events), 114 thousand ROOT files (4 billion events), and 1 million ROOT files (39 billion events), respectively. After extracting features, we build inverted indexes of trillions of events. The event indexes contain seven features, including EntryID (ID of event file), runID (ID of run), eventID (ID of global event experiment), totalCharged (total number of charged particles), totalNeutral (total number of neutral particles), totalTrks (total number of tracks) and the original ROOT file name. Then we build secondary index and import them into HBase and MySQL, respectively.

3.2   Chosen Workloads

For workloads selection, we choose typical workloads from high-energy physics. In high-energy physics, the data scale is very large, which can be achieved to petabytes scale even in one experiment. Generally, one physical analysis task only involves in a few events and the data retrieval occupies a large proportion of HEP data processing. Among them, select query is the most common requests. In high-energy physics scenario, researchers often use select query with some filter conditions to get a much smaller data set for further analysis. The select queries for MySQL and HBase used in this paper are shown as below:

```
### MySQL Query
SELECT * FROM index_tables WHERE rowkey
BETWEEN query_row_start AND query_row_stop;


### HBase Query
for key, data in table.scan(query_row_start,
query_row_stop):
    print key,data
```

3.3   Workload Generator

Since the procedure of obtaining inverted indexes from HDFS is identical, we only evaluate the procedure of querying indexes from databases. The workload generator is designed based on the principle of YCSB [6]. Analogously, we deploy a workload generator client to generate the queries according to specific arriving rates and query numbers. Our workload generator starts multiple client threads simultaneously, each sending a series of consecutive queries to access the data stored. Threads limit the rate at which they generate queries so that we can directly control the load provided by the database [10]. Threads also measure the latency of their operations and the throughput of their implementations, and report these measurements to the statistical module. At the end of the experiment, the statistical module aggregates the measurements and reports the average, maximum, minimum, and 95th percentile delays in a histogram or time series fashion.

3.4 Metrics

The evaluation use three kind of categories of metrics. User-observed performance [14] is the first one, which are easily observed and understood by users, including throughput and latency. Among them, the throughput statistics the amount of RPS, requests-per-second, and the latency counts the time spent from sending a query to receiving the result successfully. The second category is system metrics [16], we choose CPU utilization, I/O wait ratio, memory bandwidth to analyze the OS activity, respectively. The third category is micro-architecture metrics [9], which are mainly exploited by architecture research. We choose a wide range of metrics that cover all major features, including instructions per cycle, cache behaviors, branch prediction and operation intensity [11]. Table 1 summarizes all the metrics we evaluated.

Table 1. Chosen metrics.

Category	Metric name	Description
User-observed performance	Throughput	The number of processed requests per second
	Latency	The response time of each individual query
System metrics	CPU utilization	The usage of CPU resources
	I/O wait ratio	Time waiting for I/O completion
	Memory Bandwidth	The bandwidth of memory used for read/write
Micro-architecture metrics	IPC	The number of instructions executed per cycle
	Cache behaviors	Cache misses per kilo instructions
	Branch prediction	Branch miss prediction ratio
	Operation intensity	Integer computation to memory access ratio

3.5 Experimental Setup

Hardware Configurations. In our experiments, we used 32 GB memory and two Intel Xeon E5645 (Westmere) processors on the node. The CPU has six physically out-of-order and speculative pipelines kernels. There are private L1 and L2 caches in each node, and L3 caches are shared by all cores. Table 2 shows the main configurations of the processor.

Software Configurations. We deploy pseudo-distributed Hadoop [1] and HBase environment to run all workloads. For comparison, we deploy MySQL database on the same node. The operating system is Linux Ubuntu 16.04 with the 4.4.0 Linux kernel. The version of Hadoop, HBase, MySQL and JDK is 2.7.1, 1.2.6, 5.7.22 and 1.8.0, respectively.

Table 2. Details of hardware configurations.

CPU	Intel ®Xeon E5645
# Sockets	2
# Threads	12 threads
# Cores	6 cores@2.4G
L1-DCache	8-way associative, 32 KB, 64-byte per line
L1-ICache	4-way associative, 32 KB, 64-byte per line
L2 Cache	8-way associative, 256 KB, 64-byte per line
L3 Cache	16-way associative, 12 MB, 64-byte per line
Memory	32 GB, DDR3

4   Experiments and Analysis

In this section, we compare HBase and MySQL for HEP processing, from the perspectives of user-observed performance, system behaviors and micro-architecture behaviors [8]. Moreover, we use the above three data sets to evaluate their performance with various data scales, which are 0.25 million, 2.5 million, and 25 million index entries, respectively. In the following section, we use small, medium and large to represent three data scale configurations.

4.1   User-Observed Performance

In terms of user-observed performance, we analyze the throughput and latency of HBase and MySQL.

Throughput. Figure 2 shows the throughput of HBase and MySQL, which means every second the number of queries returned successfully. We consider a query as a successful one only when its response time is no more than 1 s. Figure 2 shows that HBase has a higher throughput than MySQL in three data sizes. With the expansion of data scale, HBase preserves high and steady throughput, while

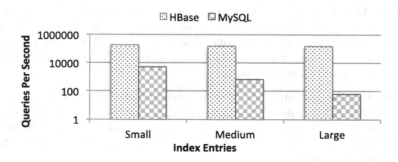

Fig. 2. Throughput.

the throughput of MySQL significantly decreases and much lower than that of HBase.

Latency. To evaluate the response latency of different systems, we analyze minimum latency, average latency, 95th percentile latency, and maximum latency through response time statistics, as shown in Fig. 3. We find that the latency of MySQL is larger than that of HBase. The minimum latency is not sensitive to the data scales in our evaluation. However, the average, maximum and 95th percentile latencies have a positive correlation with data scales. The larger the data scale is, the more response time it spends, except 95th percentile latency for HBase.

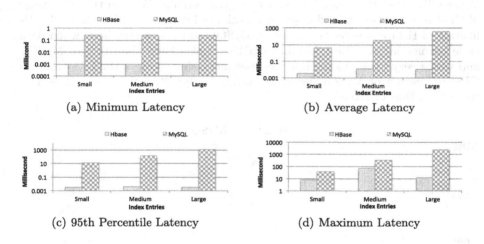

(a) Minimum Latency   (b) Average Latency

(c) 95th Percentile Latency   (d) Maximum Latency

Fig. 3. Latency.

Implications. For all three data scale configurations, the HBase's performance is better than that of MySQL, in terms of both throughput and latency. The system design decisions and storage strategies determine the performance gap between HBase and MySQL [7]. To improve the parallelism of data read and write, HBase stores the data in regions. Moreover, in each region, the data are stored consecutively in lexicographical order according to the Rowkey. However, MySQL stores data according to the writing sequence, instead of sorting by Rowkey. For HEP computing, range queries are common operations to obtain a range of data. The storage scheme of HBase can benefit range queries, since these adjacent Rowkeys are stored continuously in disk. As to MySQL, a range query always involves random data accesses, which will result in poor locality. To improve the range query performance of MySQL, we have built the indexes using B+ trees in our experiments. In summary, our experimental results show that HBase has much higher performance than MySQL for HEP scenario.

In the following sections, we will investigate the reasons of the performance difference between HBase and MySQL from both system and micro-architecture levels.

4.2 System Metrics

In terms of system metrics, we analyze the computing behaviors and memory access behaviors of workloads.

Computing Behaviors. When analyzing the computing behaviors of the workloads, we selected two CPU-related metrics: utilization of CPU and ratio of I/O waiting. The CPU utilization, which means, the proportion of running time of CPU in the total running. We can find out whether the utilization of CPU is sufficient using the metric. I/O wait ratio is the ratio of CPU time spent waiting for disk I/O to total running time of the CPU. Figures 4 and 5 shows the results of the CPU utilization and I/O wait ratio, respectively. We find that the usage of CPU resources of two index systems both are lower than 10%. The CPU utilization of HBase is lower than that of MySQL and varies very little when data scale become larger. The I/O wait of HBase is also lower than that of MySQL and varies very little. As the index entries increasing, both of the I/O wait and CPU utilization of MySQL increases. Overall, MySQL suffers from more I/O waits than that of HBase.

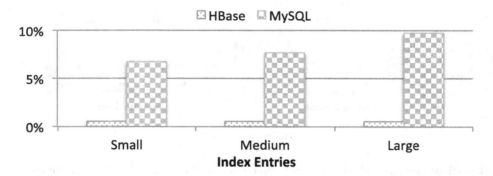

Fig. 4. CPU utilization.

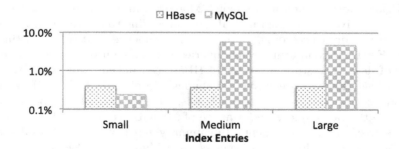

Fig. 5. I/O wait ratio.

Memory Access Behaviors. To evaluate the memory access behaviors, we choose memory bandwidth as evaluation metric. Memory bandwidth is defined as the amount of data read from the memory and data written to the memory per second. Figure 6 shows the memory bandwidth of two event index systems. We find that the memory bandwidth of HBase-based system is very low, about 10 MB/s, for all three data scale configurations. However, the memory bandwidth of MySQL is very high compared to HBase. And with increasing data scale, the memory bandwidth of MySQL increases. In HEP scenarios, the index systems have low bandwidth requirements.

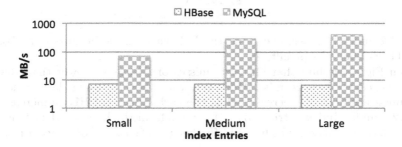

Fig. 6. Memory bandwidth.

4.3   Micro-architecture Metrics

In terms of micro-architecture metrics, we analyze instruction concurrency, locality, branch prediction and operation intensity.

Instruction Concurrency. We use the IPC (instructions per cycle) to evaluate the execution performance, which is defined as the mean of instructions per clock cycle executed. IPC is a useful metric measuring the instruction level parallelism, indicating the number of instructions are executed simultaneously. The theoretical IPC of our processors is 4. However, the actual IPC can be limited by dependencies of data or instructions and pipeline stalls. Figure 7 shows the IPC of both HBase and MySQL with different data scales. As the data scale increases, the IPC of MySQL, which is higher than that of HBase, decreases. The IPC of both systems are low (less than 0.4), due to the massive frontend and backend stalls. As the data scale increases, L3 cache miss increases, which results in the decrease of the IPC of MySQL.

Locality. Each core of the processor in our experiments is equipped with private L1 and L2 cache, and the L1 cache is further split into data cache (L1D) and instruction cache (L1I). To comprehensively understand the cache behaviors of these two index systems, we characterize the MPKI (misses per kilo-instructions)

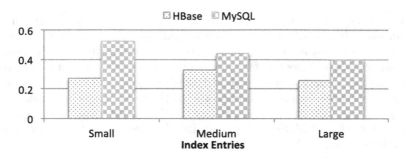

Fig. 7. IPC.

of L1I, L2 and L3 caches, excluding the L1D cache miss, because out-of-order cores [11] can belie its penalties.

From Fig. 8, we find that all cache misses of HBase are lower than that of MySQL, except L2 cache miss. Moreover, with the increasing data scale, the cache misses of MySQL decrease, while the cache misses of HBase increase. So with 0.25 million index entries, MySQL suffers from the highest L1 instruction, L2 and L3 cache misses, which would further impact its performance a lot.

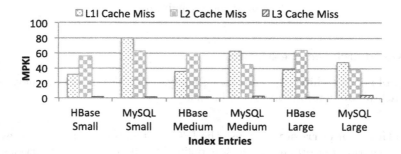

Fig. 8. Cache behaviors.

Branch Prediction. To enhance the running performance, modern processors use the branch prediction unit to predict the next instruction, so as to reduce the pipeline stalls. The prediction accuracy has a great impact on pipeline efficiency. If the prediction were wrong, the pipeline has to flush the decoded wrong instructions and fetch the correct instruction, and this would incur more penalties. Figure 9 presents the branch misprediction ratios of HBase and MySQL. The misprediction ratio of HBase is about 3% and varies very little with different data scale configurations. Moreover, the misprediction ratio of MySQL decreases with increasing data scale. Overall, MySQL owns a worse branch prediction ratio compared to HBase when data scale is larger than 2.5 millions. In summary, the misprediction ratio is relatively low, indicating that the branch prediction unit is efficient.

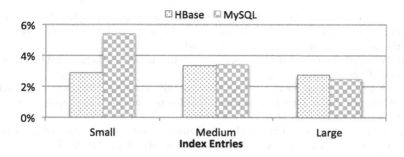

Fig. 9. Branch prediction.

Operation Intensity. Operation intensity reflects the computation pattern of a workload. It is the ratio of computation to memory accesses [14]. The experimental results show that the operation intensity of MySQL is lower than that of HBase, for all three data scale configurations. The result indicates that MySQL is more memory intensive than HBase, which means MySQL has higher memory access requirements.

5 Conclusion

The work we introduce above analyze the process of high-energy physics and propose our evaluation of two index systems of high-energy physics. We first choose representative data sets and workloads of high-energy physics. Then we select three categories of metrics to evaluate two typical index systems for HEP data management. HBase divides the data into different regions to ensure the parallelism of read and write. And each region stores rowkey in lexicographical order and stores data recently accessed into memstore. As for MySQL, the disk block is read continuously during the query. Therefore, with the data scale increasing, HBase achieves higher performance than MySQL from the perspectives of throughput and latency. Overall, HBase is more suitable for high-energy physics, which has a large data scale.

Acknowledgment. Our work in this paper is supported by NKRDPC, the National Key Research and Development Plan of China. (Grant No. 2016YFB1000600 and 2016YFB1000601).

References

1. Hadoop. http://hadoop.apache.org/
2. Hbase. https://hbase.apache.org/
3. Mysql. https://www.mysql.com/
4. Root. https://root.cern.ch/
5. Brun, R., Rademakers, F.: Root-an object oriented data analysis framework. Nucl. Instrum. Methods Phys. Res. Sect. A **389**(1–2), 81–86 (1997)

6. Cooper, B.F., Silberstein, A., Tam, E., Ramakrishnan, R., Sears, R.: Benchmarking cloud serving systems with YCSB. In: Proceedings of the 1st ACM Symposium on Cloud computing, pp. 143–154. ACM (2010)
7. Gao, W., et al.: Data motif-based proxy benchmarks for big data and AI workloads. In: IISWC 2018 (2018)
8. Gao, W., et al.: Data motifs: a lens towards fully understanding big data and AI workloads. In: 2018 27th International Conference on Parallel Architectures and Compilation Techniques (PACT) (2018)
9. Jia, Z., et al.: Characterizing and subsetting big data workloads. In: 2014 IEEE International Symposium on Workload Characterization (IISWC), pp. 191–201. IEEE (2014)
10. Jia, Z., et al.: Understanding big data analytics workloads on modern processors. IEEE Trans. Parallel Distrib. Syst. **28**(6), 1797–1810 (2017)
11. Karkhanis, T.S., Smith, J.E.: A first-order superscalar processor model. In: 31st Annual International Symposium on Computer Architecture, Proceedings, pp. 338–349. IEEE (2004)
12. Liu, B., et al.: High performance computing activities in hadron spectroscopy at BESIII. J. Phys. Conf. Ser. **523**, 012008 (2014)
13. Vora, M.N.: Hadoop-HBase for large-scale data. In: 2011 International Conference on Computer Science and Network Technology (ICCSNT), vol. 1, pp. 601–605. IEEE (2011)
14. Wang, L., et al.: Bigdatabench: a big data benchmark suite from internet services. In: 2014 IEEE 20th International Symposium on High Performance Computer Architecture (HPCA), pp. 488–499. IEEE (2014)
15. Yaodong, C., et al.: Data management challenges and event index technologies in high energy physics. J. Comput. Res. Dev. **54**(2), 258–266 (2017)
16. Zheng, C., Zhan, J., Jia, Z., Zhang, L.: Characterizing OS behaviors of datacenter and big data workloads. In: 2016 IEEE 18th International Conference on High Performance Computing and Communications; IEEE 14th International Conference on Smart City; IEEE 2nd International Conference on Data Science and Systems (HPCC/SmartCity/DSS), pp. 1079–1086. IEEE (2016)

Evaluating Graph Database Systems
for Biological Data

Minghe Yu[1,2(✉)], Yaxuan Zang[1,3], Shaopeng Dai[1,2], Daoyi Zheng[1,2],
and Jinheng Li[1]

[1] Institute of Computing Technology, Chinese Academy of Sciences, Beijing, China
{yuminghe,zangyaxuan,daishaopeng,zhengdaoyi,lijinheng}@ict.ac.cn
[2] University of Chinese Academy of Sciences, Beijing, China
[3] University of Electronic Science and Technology of China, Chengdu, China

Abstract. The graph database system can express the complex relationships in the real world through the simple and intuitive description of "entities" and "relationships". Now, the graph database system is used to analyze complex relationship between entities, especially, in the scientific research field. For example, the RDF-based graph database system has been used for biological data processing. Many previous works have proved that the graph database system is very suite for biological researchers to store and analyze biological data. In this paper, we evaluate two graph database systems (Apache Jena and gStore) by the biological RDF data set, the biological RDF data set contains 10 millions pieces of data on the types of Uniport, Enzyme, Taxonomy and Gen. And we design five query workloads, which are "1-step", "2-steps(p1)", "2-steps(p2)", "union" and "filtering" and one data load workload. The metrics which we evaluated including user-observed metrics (workload execution time), system metrics (CPU utilization, I/O wait ratio and memory bandwith) and micro-architecture metrics (IPC, cache miss and branch misprediction ratio). The experiment results show that gStore performs better in complex query workloads, and Jena is more suitable for the simple ones.

Keywords: Graph database systems · Performance evaluation
Biological data

1 Introduction

The graph database system applies the graph theory to store the relationship information between entities. The most common example is to process the relationship between people in social networks. In traditional relational database system, people should create a series of tables to represent the many-to-many relationship and hold foreign keys in all of the related tables. Unlike the relational database, the graph database system is more efficient, though combining the abstract structure of nodes and relationships into joined structures, the graph database enables us to build sophisticated models.

© Springer Nature Singapore Pte Ltd. 2019
R. Ren et al. (Eds.): SDBA 2018, CCIS 911, pp. 27–42, 2019.
https://doi.org/10.1007/978-981-13-5910-1_3

For most of biological researches, querying data with keyword in text often proves to be impractical [1]. But the RDF graph provide a powerful solution to handle the problem that data are stored multiform and distributed. They represent this different types of biological data as directed graphs and relate them to biological networks. So biological researchers often used RDF graph to describe the complex structured or semi-structured data, such as protein and gene network diagram, biological relation network diagram and various entities network diagram. The graph data becomes the first choice for biological researchers to store and analyze data in the field of biological research. Many biological RDF graph data sets are emerging. Such as, UniProt, ChEMBL and Reactome launced by EBI. Researchers with knowledge about query language can access the RDF datasets.

Today, more and more graph database systems are developed and used in biological fields. But, there is no one size fits all solution. Choosing the appropriate graph database system for biological applications is a big challenge. In this paper, we evaluate two popular graph database systems (Jena and gStore) with the biological RDF data set. And we designed five query workloads, which are "1-step", "2-steps(p1)", "2-steps(p2)", "union" and "filtering" and one data load workload. We evaluate the performance of graph database systems with the user-observed metric, and give workload characteristics from the system and micro-architecture level metrics. The experiment results show that gStore performs better in complex query workloads, and Jena is more suitable for the simple ones. For example, the performance of Jena is five times better than gStore in "1-step" which is simple query and the gStore is eight times better than Jena in "union" which is complex one. The system and micro-architecture metrics give the insights to the user-observed metric. For example, memory bandwidth of simple query explained that Jena is better than gStore on the simple query. The paper described three parts: Sect. 2 explains the backgrounds, Sect. 3 presents the design of experiment, Sect. 4 discusses the result of experiment and Sect. 5 makes a conclusion.

2   Background

This section we introduce what is RDF, RDF query language and biological dataset based RDF, and we also introduce two popular graph database system who named Jena and gStore to store biological RDF data set and a Linux performance counters "perf".

2.1   The Resource Description Framework

The Resource Description Framework (RDF) is a standard for describing relationships between entities. It's based on the idea which is expressing the resources (in particular web resources) with the form suject-predicate-object, known as triples. In the triples, the subject defined the object that the triple is describing, the predicate identifies the type of property and the object is the actual value of property. Therefore, we could use the subject and object of RDF as the vertices of the graph, and the predicate as the edge of the vertex of the association graph. In general, a triples of RDF is transformed into two nodes of property graph and a connection between two nodes, or a node of the property graph and the properties of the corresponding node. We summarize them in Table 1.

Table 1. Data model of RDF

RDF property	Description
Subject	Node of property graph
Predicate	The edge of label or the property name of the node
Object	Node of property graph or the property value of the node

2.2   The Biological RDF Data Sets

In this section, we will briefly describe each data set used in the benchmarking research. For each data set, they are real standard RDF format biological data sets. We will explain these data sets in detail as follows.

UniProt: UniProt dataset is the most comprehensive library of protein resources, including protein sequence and function information, which can be linked to other resources.

Enzyme: Enzyme dataset includes information on the classification, description, chemical composition, cofactors, protein pathways and gene products of enzymes.

Taxonomy: taxonomy dataset includes biometric Kingdom, Phylum, Class, Family, Genus, Species, and scientific name which are classification of the organism.

Gene: Gene dataset includes information about the classification, description, symbols, chromosomes and gene products of genes and genomes.

2.3   The RDF Query Language

The SPARQL [5] is a query language and data access protocol for RDF. SPARQL bases on matching graph pattern instead of query the graph structure of RDF data. And it selects one or more variables that are expressed as important positions in the graphical scheme. On the other hand, by using the SPARQL client, the user can execute the query locally by transmitting the data from server, or transmitting the query to the server to remotely execute the query through the SPARQL protocol.

2.4   The Graph Database System

The graph database system is based on the graph database model which includes a lot of vertices and edges. The vertices represent the entities and the edges represent the relationship between these entities. Unlike relational database, both vertices and edges can have additional name-value pairs called properties, the vertices always has a direction, a type, a start node and an end node.

GStore [6,7] is an RDF data management system based on native graph model. Its data model consists of a lot of vertexes which connect with the subject and the object. GStore finds subgraph matches to represent a given SPARQL and incorporates a metric across all of the RDF graphs to make the query processing more quickly.

Apache Jena is special Java framework to support the related application with semantic web which consists of various APIs for managing RDF data. Apache Jena uses component named TDB to store RDF data which can provide high-performance memory property. Unlike Sesame, Apache Jena provides support for OWL which has various internal reasoners and the Pellet reasoner can be set up to work in Apache Jena.

2.5   Perf: Linux Profiling with Performance Counters

Perf is a performance profiling tool within the Linux kernel source tree. Based on the event sampling principle, it supports the performance analysis of the performance metrics related to the processor and the performance metrics of the operating system. Perf is very powerful: it can record CPU performance counters, kprobes, tracepoints and uprobes (dynamic tracing), and it also supports lightweight profiling. Perf uses CPU hardware registers to count hardware events such as instructions execution, branch prediction, cache miss and so on. Perf abstracts the functions of different hardware and samples on top of these hardware to support annotating in every task, every CPU and every workload counters [8]. So perf is often used to find performance bottlenecks and to analyze hot spot code positioning.

3   Experimental Design

This section describes our experimental design. As shown in Fig. 1, we first analyze the characteristic of the RDF graph database, then select the typical workload of load and query data from the RDF graph databases and use workload generator to simulate the users' operations. In the process of load data and query data, we use the performance monitor to get the information, such as user-observed metrics (workload execution time), system metrics (CPU utilization, I/O wait ratio and memory bandwith) and micro-architecture metrics (IPC, cache miss and branch misprediction ratio). We use the information to evaluate two typical workload which is load data and query data in the graph database.

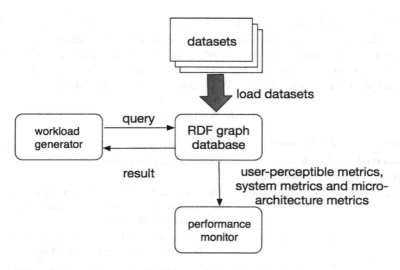

Fig. 1. Evaluation methodology

3.1   Chosen Data Set

The datasets using in experiment are real and standard biological data sets from the UniProt, Enzyme, Gene and Taxonomy, and express in RDF format. The dataset contains approximately 3.6 billion RDF triples. We extracted 10 million RDF triples from the dataset as test set. Table 2 shows some examples in the test data. In Table 2, each row represents an RDF triple, for example, the fourth row of data <A0A0E2I5D8_9LEPT, sequenceLength, "74"> respectively represents the protein number, the length of the sequence and the length of the value, and The triple denotes that the sequence length of the protein A0A0E2I5D8_9LEPT is 74.

Table 2. Examples of data sets

Subject	Predicate	Object
A0A0E2I5D8_9LEPT	type	ProteinNode
A0A0E2I5D8_9LEPT	geneId	"23005701"
A0A0E2I5D8_9LEPT	x-taxon	1049942
A0A0E2I5D8_9LEPT	sequenceLength	"74"

3.2   Metrics

We use a hierarchical analysis method to analyze the workload characteristics of the graph database from three levels. The first is user-observed characteristic analysis [9]. Users can easily observe and understand these characteristics. It is mainly the workload execution time. The second is system level characteristic analysis. The system level analyzes the dimensions of CPU utilization, I/O wait ratio and memory bandwith [10]. Third, it analyzes the characteristics of the micro-architecture level and analyzes the dimensions of IPC, cache miss, and branch misprediction ratio [11–13]. We summarize them in Table 3.

Table 3. Metrics

Category	*Metric name*	*Metric description*
User-observed metrics	Workload execution time	The time of execution
System metrics	CPU utilization	The ratio of the CPU's execution time to the total workload runtime in both user state and kernel state
	I/O wait ratio	The ratio of the CPU's time spent waiting for disk I/O to the total CPU time
	Memory bandwith	The amount at which data can be read from or stored into a memory per unit time
Micro-architecture metrics	IPC	The average number of instructions completed per clock cycle
	Cache miss	Cache misses per 1000 instructions
	Branch misprediction ratio	The ratio of branch misses

3.3 Workloads Description

In this paper, we choose two typical operations which is load and query data. Then we use performance analysis tool named "perf" to obtain the system performance metrics and analyze its user-observed metrics, system metrics and micro-architecture metrics. The experiment is composed of two parts: load operations and query operations.

- Load Operations: We import the data into the graph database and measure the performance. First, We extracted 10 million RDF triples from the UniProt, Enzyme, Gene and Taxonomy dataset as test sets, and respectively load data into Jena and gStore graph database, then we obtain performance metrics by "perf" about load data.
- Query Operations: The second part measures the effect of different query workloads on the graph databases' performance. First, we extracted 10 million RDF triples from the UniProt, Enzyme, Gene and Taxonomy dataset as test sets. Then, we consider the distribution of users query access patterns. We designed two types of access patterns. The first type of access pattern is base on the steps of "jump", the access pattern can be divided into "1-step", "2-steps(p1)" and "2-steps(p2)". The second type of access pattern are "union" and "filtering". For "1-step", the corresponding query is to

traverse two nodes, and the order of two nodes is 1, 2. Its query statement description and query statement content are as follows:

Q1:

Query the production of enzyme numbered 1.5.1.17 in the test data.
PREFIX enzyme: <http://gcm.wdcm.org/data/gcmAnnotation1/enzyme/>
PREFIX ns: <http://gcm.wdcm.org/ontology/gcmAnnotation/v1/>
SELECT ?x WHERE {
    enzyme:1.5.1.17 ns: product ?x . }

For the "2-steps(p1)" access pattern, it traverses three nodes. The system traverses node 1 first and then traverses node 2 from node 1, then the node 3 is traversed from node 2. The query language we designed and its implications are as follows:

Q2:

Query the name of x-pathway of enzyme numbered 1.5.1.31 in the test data.
PREFIX enzyme: <http://gcm.wdcm.org/data/gcmAnnotation1/enzyme/>
PREFIX ns: <http://gcm.wdcm.org/ontology/gcmAnnotation/v1/>
SELECT ?x WHERE {
    enzyme:1.5.1.17 ns: x−pathway ?y .
    ?y ns: name ?x . }

For the "2-steps(p2)" access pattern, it also traverses three nodes. The system first traverses node 1, 2, and then back to 1, from node 1 to node 3. The query language we designed and its implications are as follows:

Q3:

Query which substances(enzymes) can product both H+ and NADH in the test data.
PREFIX ns: <http://gcm.wdcm.org/ontology/gcmAnnotation/v1/>
SELECT ?x WHERE {
?x ns:product 'H+' .
?x ns:product 'NADH' . }

Union is a union of two "1-step"queries' result, and then the union set of the query results of this"1-step" query. The query language we designed and its implications are as follows:

Q4:

Query which substances(enzymes) can product H+ or NADH in the test data.
PREFIX ns: <http://gcm.wdcm.org/ontology/gcmAnnotation/v1/>
SELECT ?x WHERE {
{ ?x ns:product 'H+' . }
UNION
{ ?x ns:product 'NADH' . } }

Filtering is a operationg, similar to"2-step(p2)" operation, which filter the result of some node according specific conditions. The query language we designed and its implications are as follows:

Q5:

Query which enzymes were created in 1978 in the test data.

PREFIX ns: <http://gcm.wdcm.org/ontology/gcmAnnotation/v1/>

SELECT ?x WHERE {

?x na:type ns:EnzymeNode .

?x ns:history ?y .

Filter(regex(str(?y), 'created 1978')) }

3.4 Experimental Configurations

For each database, we use the latest versions: gStore v.0.6 and Jena v.3.7, and deploy on same physical machine at a node. To reduce error, all the experiments were implemented using the Java interface in the graph databases. And for configuring each database, we use the default configuration and recommendations found in the documentation of the websites. Experimental datasets are 10 million RDF triples from the biological data sets, its data volume is about 1.6GB. During the experiment, we submitted all of the queries one bye one, and we repeated the query workload 10,000 times and the data load workload 100 times, and obtained the average value as the evaluation metrics. The experimental platform is Intel Xeon E5645 and 96GB memory platform. We summarize them in Table 4.

Table 4. Server configurations

Processor	Intel(R) Xeon(R) CPU E5645 @ 2.4GHz
The number of core	12
Memory capacity	96 GB, DDR3
ITLB	4-way set associative, 64 entries
DTLB	4-way set associative, 64 entries
L1 DCache	32 KB
L1 ICache	32 KB
L2 Cache	256 KB
L3 Cache	12 MB
Disk capacity	1024 GB
Kernel	Linux kernel 4.13
Operating system	Ubuntu 14.04

4   Experimental Analysis

4.1   The User-Observed Characteristic Analysis

In the aspect of user-observed level characteristic analysis, we mainly analyze the characteristic of workload from the time when the load sets up the databases and the response time of a single SPARQL query.

Workload Execution Time. Workload execution time is one of the important metrics to measure the quality of graph database system. When execution environment and test data are the same in every graph database, The shorter execution time shows this graph database system workload's operation efficiency is higher and make full use of system resources. At the same time, the user's experience of the graph database system workload is better.

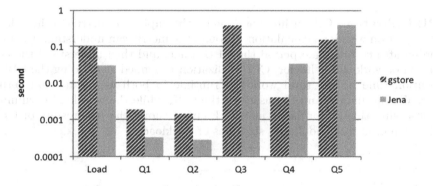

Fig. 2. Workload execution time

It is shown in Fig. 2 using a logarithmic scale for execution time that the average execution time of the six types of workloads. As shown in the figure, gStore uses far less time than Jena when executing the load, Q1, Q2 and Q3 workloads and uses far longer time when executing the Q4 and Q5 workloads, which indicates that gStore performs worse than Jena when running the load, Q1, Q2 and Q3 workloads, and better than Jena when running the Q4 and Q5 workloads.

After analysis, we found that the load, Q1, Q2 and Q3 workloads respectively belong to load data workloads and n-steps (Q1, Q2 and Q3) type of simple query workloads, the Q4 and Q5 workloads respectively belong to complex query workload of the union and filter. This indicates that Jena performs better than gStore in load data workload and simple query workload of n-steps type, and weaker than gStore in complex query workload of union and filter.

On the other hand, we found that gStore established a deep balance tree during the load data workload process, while Jena just established a common index. Because it takes much longer to set up a deep balance tree than to set up a common index, the load data workload's execution time in the gStore is much longer than Jena's workload. And in terms of query workload, gStore in the process of query uses a deep balance tree and a lot of cutting algorithm to accelerate the subgraph query, so query time in Q4, Q5 of gStore is shorter than the Jena. Using deep balance tree and cutting algorithm needs a lot of time and space. So in execution Q1, Q2 and Q3 simple query workload, gStore uses longer time rather than the Jena.

In conclusion, gStore performs better in complex query workload, and Jena is more suitable for simple query workload than gStore.

4.2   Characteristic Analysis in System Level

In terms of system level characteristic analysis, we will analyze the three dimensions of workload: CPU utilization, I/O waiting ratio and memory bandwidth.

CPU Utilization. CPU utilization is one of the important metrics of the behavior of reaction workload calculation, through the metric can understand the load running at a certain time period the CPU usage, and then understand the calculation of workload behavior. CPU utilization is defined as dividing the CPU's execution time by the total workload runtime in both user state and kernel state. We can understand the usage of the CPU while the workload is running by observing this performance metric. Figure 3 shows the test results of CPU utilization of gStore and Jena's six types of workload.

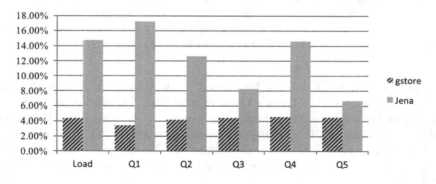

Fig. 3. CPU utilizaton

It is seen from the figure that gStore CPU utilization is about 4%, Jena CPU utilization fluctuates between 6% and 18%, which means gStore and Jena workload calculation behavior is quite different. Jena's calculation behavior is more sensitive with six types of workload while gStore is not sensitive with queries.

I/O Wait Ratio. I/O wait ratio is the another important metrics to calculate reaction workload behavior, through the observation of workload I/O wait ratio, we can understand whether the workload affect the calculation of workload behavior by waiting the I/O. The I/O wait ratio is defined as divide the ratio of the CPU's time spend waiting for disk I/O by the total CPU time. By observing the I/O wait ratio, we can understand whether the workload affects the use of the CPU by waiting for disk I/O during execution.

The test results of I/O wait ratios of gStore and Jena's six types of workload are shown in Fig. 4.

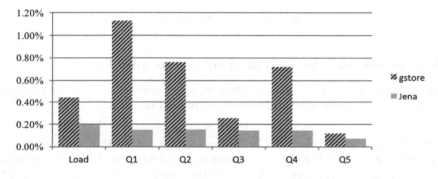

Fig. 4. I/O wait ratio

In terms of I/O wait, the I/O wait ratio of each workload is not high which between 0.24% to 1%. This implied that disk I/O is not the bottleneck of gStore and Jena under our experiments.

Memory Bandwidth. Memory is the most frequently used part of the entire computer system, and almost every operation has to pass through memory. In this way, the performance of memory bandwidth determines the performance of the system. Through observing the memory bandwidth, we can clearly understand the workload storage requirements, and then analyze the workload performance. Memory bandwidth is defined as the amount of read/write data in memory per unit of time.

Figure 5 shows the memory bandwidth test results for gStore and Jena's query and load data workloads. As can be seen from the figure, there is a obvious difference from query workload and load workload which is the highest value of 240 KB/s and the lowest value of 5 KB/s. In Q1 and Q2 workloads, memory bandwidth of the gStore is far higher than the Jena while in the Q4, Q5 workloads, gStore is lower than Jena. This lead to the execution time of gStore in Q1 and Q2 workloads is shorter than Jena. In Q4, Q5 workloads gStore is longer than Jena in execution time.

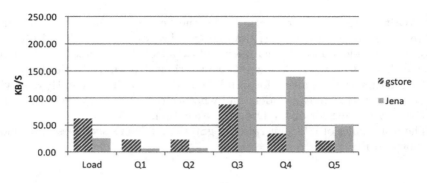

Fig. 5. Memory bandwidth

4.3   Characteristic Analysis in Micro-architecture Level

In micro-architectural level characteristic analysis, we will analyze three dimensions of the IPC, cache miss and branch misprediction ratio.

Instructions Per Cycle (IPC). For analyzing instruction concurrency in workloads, we select IPC as the performance. The definition of IPC (instructions per cycle) is the average number of instructions completed per clock cycle. IPC is an important metric for evaluating the micro-architecture performance in the system.

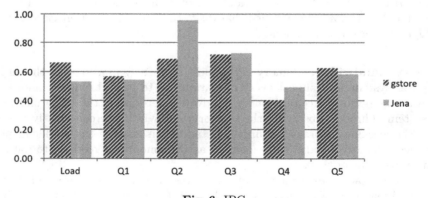

Fig. 6. IPC

Figure 6 shows the concurrency of all the instructions loaded by gStore and Jena. As can be seen from the figure, each workload of gStore is similar to the instruction concurrency of Jena's workload, so IPC is not the main factor affecting performance.

Cache Miss. Cache is a high-speed buffer storage in computer and is where data and instructions are cached. Current processors are memory hierarchy architecture, which use a cache between the processor and memory to reduce the CPU's latency. We can analyze the cache miss to understand the locality of the workload in terms of fetching data and instructions. The lower the numbers of cache miss, the better the locality of the program and vice versa.

We use a three-level cache in the experiment, in which each physical core has an independent L1 Cache and an L2 Cache, and all physical cores share the L3 Cache. The L1 Cache is divided into a L1 Instruction Cache and a L1 Data Cache. The capacity of the L1 Cache is small and the access latency time is short. The L2 Cache has a greater capacity than the L1 Cache, but the latency time is longer. The L3 Cache is the largest capacity and the longest latency time. We do not analyze the L1 Data Cache because its accuracy is affected by out-of-order execution [14]. On the other hand, the L3 Cache is shared by all the physical core, the locality is more ambiguous than L1 Cache and L2 Cache. So we will analyze the cache behavior of the L1 Instruction Cache and L2 Cache.

From the test results, we found that the L1 Instruction Cache miss and L2 Cache miss in query workloads (Q1, Q2, Q3, Q4 and Q5) of the gStore and Jena are similar, in which the L1 Instruction Cache miss of the query workload is about 30 per 1000 instructions and L2 Instruction Cache miss is about 40 per 1000. So the L1 Instruction Cache miss and L2 Cache miss are not factors that affect the gStore and Jena query workload. However, the L1 instruction Cache miss of the load data workload between gStore and Jena is much different, gStore is approximately 3 per 1000 instructions and Jena is approximately 10 per 1000 instructions. The load data workload of the gStore is significantly superior in the L1 Instruction Cache miss. But in execution time, gStore's load data load execution time is significantly worse than Jena. After analysis, we found that the data load workload execution process mainly loads data from the hard disk into the memory. For more discussion, the behavior of the instruction cache (L1 Instruction Cache) has little impact on the workload and cannot be a key factor influencing the data load workload.

Branch Misprediction Ratio. Branch prediction is a method used by modern processors to increase CPU execution speed which predicts the branch flow of the program, and then reads and decodes one of the branch instructions in advancing to reduce the time to wait for the decoder, which correspondingly improves the overall execution speed of the CPU. Waiting for the result and then executing the new instructions has extra cycle consumption, making the execution efficiency of the pipeline lower. In analyzing the branch prediction characteristics of the workload, we choose branch misprediction ratio as the evaluation metric. On the other hand, once the result of the previous instruction proves that the branch prediction is wrong, in other word, the wrong branch prediction has occurred, the instructions and results already loaded into the pipeline must be completely removed and then the correct instruction must be loaded. In this way, there is extra cycle consumption compared to not performing branch prediction but waiting for the result and then executing the new instruction, making the execution efficiency of the pipeline lower. In analyzing the branch prediction characteristics of the workload, we choose branch misprediction ration as the performance metric.

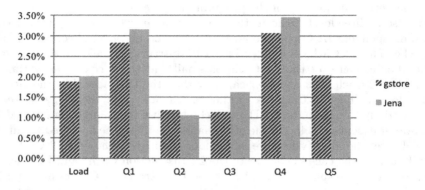

Fig. 7. Branch miss

The prediction precision of branch instruction is one of the important factors that directly affect the performance. Figure 7 shows the branch misprediction ratio in the gStore and Jena workloads. It is can be seen in the figure that the branch misprediction ratio in gStore workload and Jena workload is similar, so the branch misprediction ratio is not the reason to affect the performance difference between gStore and Jena. On the other hand, the branch misprediction ratio in gStore workload and Jena workload is as high as 3.5%, the lowest was 1.2%, and in general all branch misprediction ratio is very low, because six types workload of branching logic code is simple, branching behavior with great regularity. The low error rate for six types of workloads indicates that most of branch instructions in the workload have simple patterns. The simple patterns help BTB (branch target buffer) predict whether the next branch will need to jump, which may be the reason for their low bit error rate.

4.4   Summary

We analyse the characteristic of six types workload in gStore and Jena from user-observed level, system level and micro-architecture level. We also analyse six metrics which are CPU utilization, I/O wait ratio, memory bandwidth, IPC, cache miss and branch misprediction ratio. It is found that the first three metrics have a great influence on performance of the workloads, while the last three metrics have a litter influence on performance of the workloads.

5   Conclusion

In this article, we use 10 million of RDF biological data to evaluate two graph database systems (Apache Jena and gStore), we designed five types of query workload and one type of load data workload in the process of evaluation, the experiment results show that the Jena in load data workload and a simple query workload (Q1 and Q2, Q3) execution has a higher efficiency than gStore workloads, while the Jena in complex query workload (Q4, Q5) has a less execution efficiency than gStore workloads.

After analysis, we found gStore will establish a depth balance tree in the process of load data, and because establishing a depth balance tree needs a lot of time, so the efficiency of gStore to execute load data workload is lower than the Jena. On the other hand, owing to use depth balance tree to search and use a lot of cutting algorithm to accelerate the subgraph query, gStore has a higher efficiency than the Jena in complex query workload (Q4, Q5), and gStore needs a lot of time and space overhead to support depth balance tree and cutting algorithm, so gStore has a lower efficiency. Then we analyze the workload characteristic from the system-level (CPU utilization, I/O wait ratio, memory bandwidth), micro-architecture (IPC branch misprediction ratio and cache miss) and show the six types of gStore and Jena from multiple perspectives and analyze the reasons affecting the efficiency of the workload execution. Analysis shows that CPU utilization, I/O wait ratio, and memory bandwidth have a great influence on the operating efficiency of the six types of workloads, while IPC, cache miss and branch misprediction ratio have almost no effect on operating efficiency.

Acknowledgment. This work is supported by the National Key Research and Development Plan of China (Grant No.2016YFB1000600 and 2016YFB1000601).

References

1. De Virgilio, R., Rombo, S.E.: Approximate matching over biological RDF graphs. 1413–1414 (2012)
2. Consortium U P: UniProt: a hub for protein information. Nucleic Acids Res. **43**(Database issue), 204–212 (2015)
3. UniProt Consortium: UniProt: the universal protein knowledgebase. Nucleic Acids Res. **45**(D1), D158–D169 (2016)
4. Duan, S., Kementsietsidis, A., Srinivas, K., et al.: Apples and oranges: a comparison of RDF benchmarks and real RDF datasets. In: Proceedings of the 2011 ACM SIGMOD International Conference on Management of Data, pp. 145-156. ACM (2011)
5. Prud'Hommeaux, E., Seaborne, A.: SPARQL query language for RDF, W3C Recommendation (2008)
6. Zou, L., Özsu, M.T., Chen, L., et al.: gStore: a graph-based SPARQL query engine. VLDB J. Int. J. Very Large Data Bases **23**(4), 565–590 (2014)
7. Zeng, L., Zou, L.: Redesign of the gStore system. Front. Comput. Sci. **2**, 1–19 (2018)
8. https://perf.wiki.kernel.org/index.php/Main_Page

9. Wang, L., et al.: Bigdatabench: a big data benchmark suite from internet services. In: 2014 IEEE 20th International Symposium on High Performance Computer Architecture (HPCA). IEEE (2014)
10. Zheng, C., Zhan, J., Jia, Z., et al.: Characterizing OS behaviors of datacenter and big data workloads. In: 2016 IEEE 18th International Conference on High Performance Computing and Communications; IEEE 14th International Conference on Smart City; IEEE 2nd International Conference on Data Science and Systems (HPCC/SmartCity/DSS), pp. 1079-1086. IEEE (2016)
11. Jia, Z., Zhan, J., Wang, L., et al.: Characterizing and subsetting big data workloads. In: 2014 IEEE International Symposium on Workload Characterization (IISWC), pp. 191–201. IEEE (2014)
12. Gao, W., Zhan, J., Wang, L., et al.: Data Motifs: A Lens Towards Fully Understanding Big Data and AI Workloads. IEEE Parallel Architectures and Compilation Techniques (2018)
13. Gao, W., Zhan, J., Wang, L., et al.: Data Motif-based Proxy Benchmarks for Big Data and AI Workloads. IISWC (2018)
14. Jia, Z., Zhan, J., Wang, L., et al.: Understanding big data analytics workloads on modern processors. IEEE Trans. Parallel Distrib. Syst. **28**(6), 1797–1810 (2017)

Performance Optimization

WASC: Adapting Scheduler Configurations for Heterogeneous MapReduce Workloads

Siyi Wang[1], Fan Zhang[2(✉)], and Rui Han[2]

[1] Zhengzhou University, Zhengzhou, China
wangsiyi@zzu.edu.cn
[2] Institute of Computing Technology,
Chinese Academy of Sciences, Beijing, China
{zhangfan,hanrui}@ict.ac.cn

Abstract. MapReduce has emerged as a popular programming paradigm for data intensive computing in both scientific and commercial applications. On a MapReduce cluster, modern resource negotiation frameworks like Hadoop YARN and Mesos support scheduling of jobs submitted by multiple tenants. However, existing job schedulers lacks the automatic adaption to workload variations in their scheduling configuration, which is crucial for the jobs' latencies because it determines how to share resources among the latest jobs in the system. The major challenge here is, to a MapReduce cluster scheduler, The performance of different configurations depends not only on the number of jobs in different queues, but also on their workload characteristics, which refer to the type and size of jobs. We introduce a workload-adaptive scheduling configuration (WASC) framework for heterogeneous MapReduce jobs. WASC identifies the optimal configuration for them by reasoning about their performances under different configurations.

Keywords: MapReduce · Workload heterogeneous
Cluster schedulers · Configurations

1 Introduction

MapReduce is a prevalent parallel programming model that is widely used to process data-intensive applications such as scientific data analyses whose data are collected from various instruments [16]. Modern resource scheduling like Hadoop YARN (Yet Another Resource Negotiator) [2] and Mesos [1] provide the flexible resource sharing mechanism for MapReduce jobs. This promotes emerging trends that jobs submitted by different application users are organized in the multi-tenancy form (where multiple tenants share the same cluster) to increase the cost-effectiveness, besides, increases complexity of the cluster management.

Figure 1 illustrates a typical Hadoop YARN scheduler, which uses a hierarchy of queues to share resources in multi-tenancy cluster [9]. The two-level job

© Springer Nature Singapore Pte Ltd. 2019
R. Ren et al. (Eds.): SDBA 2018, CCIS 911, pp. 45–54, 2019.
https://doi.org/10.1007/978-981-13-5910-1_4

scheduler allows MapReduce jobs of different organizations (user departments) to share resources using the first-level queues (e.g. q_1 and q_n), while employing the second-level queues (e.g. q_{11} and q_{12}) to manage jobs of different applications such as scientific analyses in high energy physics and astronomy and internet services. This paper focuses on the scheduling of jobs in a second-level queue (i.e. jobs of an organization), in which two hierarchical **scheduling configuration parameters** control the assignment of available resources among a mix of jobs from different tenants [7]: (1) a *resource sharing parameter among queues* decides the ratio of resources allocated to different queues; and (2) a *scheduling policy within queues* decides the resource allocation among the jobs within the same queue. For example, the Capacity [4] and Fair scheduler [5] are widely used to allocate shared resource among queues, and the commonly used scheduling policies on YARN are Fair, Dominant Resource Fairness (DRF) [12], and first-in-first-out (FIFO).

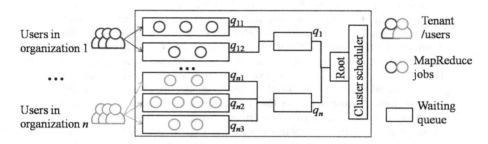

Fig. 1. Scheduling of multi-tenant MapReduce jobs on a Hadoop cluster

Hence given a MapReduce cluster scheduler, on the one hand, the choice of scheduling configurations significantly affects the performances of jobs because each configuration corresponds to a different resource allocation and distinct execution order. Existing cluster schedulers for MapReduce jobs, whether cited in literatures (e.g. Natjam [10] and Phurti [8]) or used in production system (e.g. YARN and Mesos) depend on cluster operators to change the schedulers' configurations mannually [6]. But in a multi-tenant MapReduce cluster, the performance of different configurations and the optimal configuration vary not only depending on the numbers of jobs in different queues, but also these jobs' workload characteristics,which is reflected by their job input data sizes and types. [9,14,15], as shown in Table 1.

In this paper, we address the challenge of identify optimal configuration of MapReduce job scheduling by proposing WASC, a framework that adapts the configuration of a given scheduler to the different mix of jobs in the system. The identification is based on a mix of job scheduling simulation and model-based estimation of these jobs' performances. Specifically, the simulation of a configuration predicts the resource assignments to the candidate jobs under this configuration and further estimates the latency of each job according to its work-load characteristic and resource assignment. Note that WASC is not intend to replace, but rather complement the existing MapReduce job schedulers by adapt-ing their configurations to the heterogenous workloads. WASC also differs from the techniques that optimize the Hadoop configuration parameters for *individ-ual* MapReduce programs [13]. In contrast, WASC focuses on optimizing the scheduling configuration of *a mix of jobs* in multi-tenant scenarios.

WASC features on handling mixes of jobs under the empirical observation that setting different configuration parameters in a job scheduler significantly impacts the performances of the jobs.

2   Motivating Examples

WASC features on handling mixes of jobs under the empirical observation that setting different configuration parameters in a job scheduler significantly impacts the performances of the jobs. Within this context, this section shows the different workload characteristics of MapReduce jobs and their dynamicity in production systems. Within this context, we further demonstrate how different scheduling configurations influence the performances of MapReduce jobs on a testbed of Hadoop cluster, and present the key challenge to be addressed in workload-adaptive scheduling configuration.

MapReduce Jobs in Production Hadoop Systems. We analyzed the work-load characteristics of MapReduce jobs in four production traces containing 73,836 to 2,298,377 MapReduce jobs, as listed in Table 1. The analysis results show: A Hadoop cluster is shared by tenants of several application domains (e.g. interactive queires, graph and text data analyses, and system data processing). The workloads in each domain can be represented by a list of common job types (e.g. select, insert, aggregate, and transform in Hive queries, or text classification and naive Bayes in data analyses). Each job type has a wide range of input data sizes ranging from KB to TB.

Hence, different job types are better suited by different configurations and there isn't *one-size-fits-all optimal scheduling configuration under heterogeneous workloads*. To illustrate this, we present an example of scheduling MapReduce jobs on a Hadoop YARN cluster using the Capacity and Fair schedulers. In this example, we use the MapReduce jobs generated by SWIM [3], and use a job's *latency*, including both its queueing delay and the time of be processed, to represent its *performance*.

Evaluation Settings. Two clusters of different resource capacities, namely six and eight containers (each container has 2GB memory and 1 CPU core), are considered here. Both schedulers employ two queues, called q_A and q_B, to share resources among jobs. The *Capacity* scheduler supports allocation of resource capacities to different queues. For the cluster of six containers, there are five configurations in this scheduler, where configuration c_i ($1 \leq i \leq 5$) allocates i containers to q_A and ($6-i$) containers to q_B, and the scheduling policy applied in both queues is FIFO. Similarly, for the cluster of eight containers, this scheduler has seven configurations. In both clusters, nine scheduling configurations c_1 to c_9 (listed in Table 2) are applied in the *Fair* scheduler, in which queues' weights determine their resource sharing proportions and each queue supports three scheduling policies. For each configuration, we apply it to schedule the seven different mixes of MapReduce jobs on both clusters. Each mix consists of 12 Facebook jobs of different workload characteristics and resource demands.

Table 1. Workload traces of MapReduce jobs in production Hadoop systems

Trace	Statistics	Workload characteristic	
	Machines/Lengths/Jobs	Job types	Input data sizes
Facebook traces [9]	3600/7.5 months/2,298,377	Data loading, Hive queries (select, insert, aggregate, and transform), advertisement analysis	10 KB– 6.7 TB
Cloudera traces [9]	1600–1700/4 to 5 months /73,836	Pig queries (select, insert), Oozie jobs, and snapshots	4.6 KB– 7.6 TB
Yahoo! trace [14]	400/10 months/171,079	Graph and text data analyses, log analysis, and natural language processing (machine translation)	1 MB– 800 MB
Taobao trace [15]	2,000/17 days/912,157	Collaborate filtering for recommendation, analysis of traffic statistics and advertisement	1 KB– 500 TB

Table 2. Nine candidate scheduling configurations in the Fair scheduler with two queues

Configuration	c_1	c_2	c_3	c_4	c_5	c_6	c_7	c_8	c_9
q_A's weight	25	50	75	25	50	75	25	50	75
q_B's weight	75	50	25	75	50	25	75	50	25
Scheduling policy	FIFO			Fair			DRF		

Evaluation Results. The results in Table 3 list the *optimal* scheduling configuration in each test, and show the average percentage of increased latencies of each mix of jobs when comparing the *other non-optimal* configurations to the optimal one. The results show: (i) the optimal configuration varies across different mixes of jobs for the same cluster, and across different clusters for the same mix; (ii) compared to the optimal configuration, other configurations cause significant increases in job latencies (i.e. degradation in performances): the latencies are increased by an average of 123.17% for the Capacity scheduler and 18.87%

Table 3. Comparison of optimal and other configurations of the Capacity and Fair schedulers under different mixes of jobs

Mix of jobs	Cluster of six containers				Cluster of eight containers			
	Optimal configuration		Increased latency(%)		Optimal configuration		Increased latency(%)	
	Capacity	Fair	Capacity	Fair	Capacity	Fair	Capacity	Fair
1	c_5	c_1	88.91	45.50	c_5	c_1	56.03	17.97
2	c_3	c_9	60.87	11.32	c_5	c_5	49.81	15.80
3	c_5	c_1	122.42	27.93	c_6	c_3	291.02	39.25
4	c_3	c_4	113.20	8.72	c_2	c_3	285.74	4.03
5	c_3	c_4	77.68	37.42	c_2	c_9	333.77	13.85
6	c_3	c_8	77.27	11.57	c_4	c_9	49.02	11.51
7	c_3	c_1	62.78	9.27	c_3	c_5	55.87	10.02

for the Fair scheduler. These increases are up to 746.30% and 114.89% for the worst configurations in the two schedulers.

Challenge. Mainstream MapReduce scheduling frameworks such as Hadoop YARN [2] and Mesos [1] support dynamic adjustment of configurations in their schedulers. This gives an opportunity to adjust the configuration when the system workload varies. To this end, the **key challenge** is being able to efficiently reason about the impact of different *scheduling configurations* (i.e. resource assignment schemes) on the performance of jobs of different workload characteristics.

3 WASC

WASC aims to find an optimal configuration of a MapReduce scheduler according to the latest workload in the system. The available *candidate configurations* (and their parameters) depends on the specific scheduler considered. For example, the YARN Capacity scheduler allows the setting of the "Capacity" parameter to assign fixed amounts of resource to different queues. In contrast, the YARN Fair scheduler employs the "Weight" parameter to set the fractions of resource used by different queues but also allows a queue's idle resources to be assigned to other queues. Note that WASC only needs to select from a fixed and moderate number of candidate configurations for the scheduler considered because: (i) different scheduling configurations shall result into differential performances; and (ii) there are only a small number of scheduling policies within queues (e.g. FIFO, Fair and DRF) for selection.

WASC is composed of three modules that work together to conduct workload-adaptive configuration, as shown in Fig. 2. The *Job Scheduling Simulator (JSS)* module checks the latest waiting jobs in the system and estimates their latencies under all m candidate configurations, so as to select the optimal one c^* with the lowest latency. For each configuration, this module forwards it to the *Model-based Resource Assigner (MRA)* for predicting the resource assignments to the waiting jobs under c. After obtaining each job j's resource assignment a, the JSS further relays a and j to the *Job Performance Estimator (JPE)* to estimate j's running time t. Using the information of all jobs' running times, the JSS simulates the execution of these jobs and estimates their latencies under configuration c, thus selecting the optimal one c^* with the lowest latency.

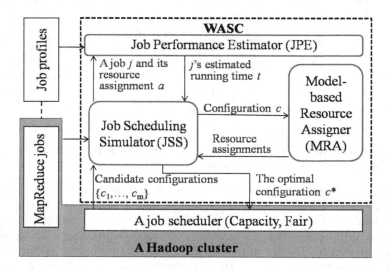

Fig. 2. The overview of WASC

We first briefly highlight the design choices of three modules, in contrast to the related work.

JPE. This module is responsible for estimating a job j's running time t under resource assignment a. Existing MapReduce performance models either consider the performance interference factors (e.g. the overlapping of map and shuffle phases, and worker and node failures [17]) in job executions, or study the large space of configuration parameters in Hadoop that may influence job performances [13]. However, these models need significant off-line profilings/learnings to incorporate different performance factors or Hadoop parameters. By contrast, WASC aims to compare the impacts of different configurations on jobs' latencies, rather than predicting their actual latencies. This means the estimation in WASC follows the assumption that each configuration is conducted under the same system environment (i.e. the same interference factors) and parameters. The JPE, therefore, needs a much simpler profiling procedure compared to existing performance models.

MRA. This module makes predictions about how to assign available resources to the waiting jobs under a scheduling configuration c. The model-based reasoning method [11] is used for two reasons. First, it creates a model of the scheduler studied, thus providing the ability to handle a variety of situations in resource assignment, including the variations in assignable resources, jobs' resource demands and configurations. Second, in WASC, each assignment only needs to consider released resources and waiting jobs within a short interval. This guarantees small search spaces in the reasoning process and thus short searching time.

JSS. This module is designed to simulate the executions of jobs under a configuration c and estimate the latencies (i.e. waiting and running times) of jobs submitted to different queues. We note that given some jobs in the queues, a queueing system model can reflect the effect of resource assignment on different queues' service times (e.g. a larger assignment leads to shorter service time), thus estimating the jobs' latencies under the assumption that the queues' service times follow some distributions (e.g. general or exponential distributions). This assumption does not hold in our scenario: queues' service times depend on the assigned resources and such an assignment changes quickly because most of the jobs have short durations and the resources are released and re-assigned once a job is completed. Hence the JSS is proposed to simulate the scheduling of waiting jobs under the fast dynamics of resource allocation.

3.1   Job Performance Estimator (JPE)

The JPE predicts a job j's running time t based on job profiles obtained from executing jobs in a staging environment or past running logs. The profiles are comprised of basic performance variants that reflect *all phases* of j, including the communication times of the input data load phase and the shuffle phase, and the computation times of individual map and reduce tasks. All these performance variants are proportion to j's input data size and we build the relationship between each variant and j's job type and input data size using regression models.

Based on job profiles, the overall estimation of job j's running time is broken down into three stages, which stepwise calculate the durations of tasks, waves, and phases in the job.

Calculation of Task Durations. The JPE first calculates the number of map tasks as j's input size divided by the block size (e.g. 128 MB) and decides all map tasks' input sizes. It then calculates the number of reduce tasks and their input sizes according to the system configuration and the shuffle size decided by j's job type and input size. Finally, it estimate all map and reduce tasks' durations (computation times) based on the constructed regression models.

Calculation of Wave Durations. The JPE decides the numbers of map and reduce waves according to j's resource assignment a. For each map or reduce wave, its duration is calculated as the maximal durations of its tasks.

Calculation of Phase Durations. For the map or reduce phases, its duration is the summation of its waves' durations. For the input data loading phase or the shuffle phase, its duration is predicted using the regression models. The JPE finally calculates j's running time t as the summation of the four sequential phases' durations.

3.2 Model-Based Resource Assigner (MRA)

In the MapReduce system, jobs of different workload characteristics usually have different resource demands. For example, a job of a larger input size usually requests more resources. Given some assignable resources, the MRA addresses the problem of allocating these resources to the waiting jobs according scheduling configuration c. In the MRA, a model is created to describe a job scheduler such that the scheduler's hierarchical configuration parameters are partitioned into a hierarchy of components in the model, as shown in Fig. 3. Based on the model, the MRA predicts the resource assignment behavior of the scheduler under configuration c from the behavior of its model components: (1) *Queue-level assignment reasoner*. This component takes the assignable resources, jobs' resource demands, and queues resource sharing parameters as inputs, and outputs the resource assignments to the k queues in the scheduler; (2) *Job-level assignment reasoner*. Each of this component corresponds to one queue and it takes the assigned resource, the jobs' resource demands, and the scheduling policy of its corresponding queue as inputs, deduces the execution orders of the jobs, and outputs the resource assignments to them.

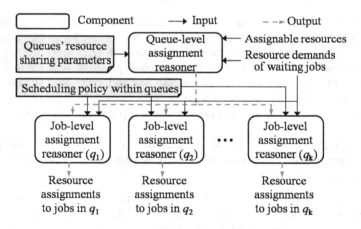

Fig. 3. Principles of model-based resource assignment

Note that the MRA is developed for typical scheduling scenarios where jobs of an application domain are either submitted to one queue (then only the *scheduling policy within queues* determines the resource assignment), or a small number of queues (e.g. less than 5 queues). When we submit diverse workloads to different queues, current scheduler usually divide them into small groups and organize them in a hierarchical structure [7]. In the case, the MRA needs to create a model with more hierarchies while still maintaining a small number of queues at each hierarchy to provide fast reasoning time.

3.3   Job Scheduling Simulator (JSS)

The steps of this module are detailed in Algorithm 1. Given the m candidate configurations of a scheduler, it periodically checks the latest set J of waiting jobs (line 1), estimates the latencies of all these jobs under each configuration (line 2 to 7), selects the optimal configuration c^* that leads to the minimal weighted latency (line 8), and returns c^* that is used to schedule jobs in next interval (line 9). Specifically, given a scheduling configuration c, the JSS first calls the MRA to predict the allocation of available resources a among the waiting jobs in J (line 3). It then calls the JPE to estimate each waiting job's latency under its resource assignment (line 4 to 6).

Algorithm 1. Job Scheduling Simulator (JSS)

Require: c: a candidate configuration;
Require: $\{c_1,...,c_m\}$: the m candidate configurations.
Require: a: the amount of available resource.
1. Obtain the set $J=\{j_1,...,j_n\}$ of waiting jobs in the system;
2. **for** $(i=1; i \leq m; i++)$ **do**
3.   Call the MRA to predict the resource assignments to the jobs in J under configuration c_i;
4.   **for** (each job j in J) **do**
5.   Call the JPE to estimate j's latency l under j's resource assignment;
6.   **end for**
7. **end for**
8. $c^*=\arg\min_{c \in C}(\sum_{j \in J_{Int}}(l \times p))$; //minimize the latency
9. Return c^*.

---

4   Summary

In this paper, we present WASC, an adaptive scheduling configuration framework for MapReduce jobs in multi-tenant Hadoop clusters. To adapt to the changing mixes of jobs of various workload characteristics, WASC estimates the latencies of the latest jobs under all candidate configurations, thus selecting the one that provides the best performance. Our future work will implement WASC on representative schedulers (e.g. YARN Fair and Capacity) and evaluate its effectiveness using workloads in real applications.

References

1. Apache mesos. http://mesos.apache.org/
2. Hadoop yarn. https://hadoop.apache.org/docs/r2.7.2/hadoop-yarn/hadoop-yarn-site/YARN.html
3. Statistical workload injector for mapreduce (swim). https://github.com/SWIMProjectUCB/SWIM/wiki

4. Yarn capacity scheduler. http://hadoop.apache.org/docs/current/hadoop-yarn/hadoop-yarn-site/CapacityScheduler.html
5. Yarn fair scheduler. http://hadoop.apache.org/docs/current/hadoop-yarn/hadoop-yarn-site/FairScheduler.html
6. Alapati, S.R.: Expert Hadoop Administration: Managing, Tuning, and Securing Spark, YARN, and HDFS. Addison-Wesley Professional, Boston (2016)
7. Bhattacharya, A.A., Culler, D., Friedman, E., Ghodsi, A., Shenker, S., Stoica, I.: Hierarchical scheduling for diverse datacenter workloads. In: SoCC 2013, p. 4. ACM (2013)
8. Cai, C.X., Saeed, S., Gupta, I., et al.: Phurti: application and network-aware flow scheduling for multi-tenant MapReduce clusters. In: IC2E 2016, pp. 161–170. IEEE (2016)
9. Chen, Y., Alspaugh, S., Katz, R.: Interactive analytical processing in big data systems: a cross-industry study of MapReduce workloads. In: VLDB 2011, vol. 5, pp. 1802–1813 (2012)
10. Cho, B., Rahman, M., Chajed, T., et al.: Natjam: design and evaluation of eviction policies for supporting priorities and deadlines in mapreduce clusters. In: SoCC 2013, p. 6. ACM (2013)
11. Davis, R., Hamscher, W.: Model-based reasoning: troubleshooting. Explor. Artif. Intell. 8, 297–346 (1988)
12. Ghodsi, A., Zaharia, M., Hindman, B., Konwinski, A., Shenker, S., Stoica, I.: Dominant resource fairness: fair allocation of multiple resource types. In: NSDI 2011, vol. 11, pp. 24–24 (2011)
13. Herodotou, H., et al.: Starfish: a self-tuning system for big data analytics. In: CIDR 2011, pp. 261–272 (2011)
14. Kavulya, S., Tan, J., Gandhi, R., Narasimhan, P.: An analysis of traces from a production MapReduce cluster. In: CCGrid 2010, pp. 94–103. IEEE (2010)
15. Ren, Z., Xu, X., Wan, J., Shi, W., Zhou, M.: Workload characterization on a production Hadoop cluster: a case study on Taobao. In: IISWC 2012, pp. 3–13. IEEE (2012)
16. Srirama, S.N., Jakovits, P., Vainikko, E.: Adapting scientific computing problems to clouds using MapReduce. Future Gener. Comput. Syst. 28(1), 184–192 (2012)
17. Verma, A., Cherkasova, L., Campbell, R.H.: ARIA: automatic resource inference and allocation for MapReduce environments. In: ICAC 2011, pp. 235–244. ACM (2011)

Asynchronous COMID: The Theoretic Basis for Transmitted Data Sparsification Tricks on Parameter Server

Cheng Daning[1,2], Li Shigang[1(✉)], and Zhang Yunquan[1]

[1] SKL of Computer Architecture, Institute of Computing Technology,
CAS, Beijing, China
{chengdaning,lishigang,zyq}@ict.ac.cn
[2] University of Chinese Academy of Sciences, Beijing, China

Abstract. Asynchronous FTRL-proximal and $L2$ norm done at server are two widely used tricks in Parameters Server which is an implement of delayed SGD. Their commonness is leaving parts of updating computation on server which reduces the burden of network via making transmitted data sparse. But above tricks' convergences are not well-proved. In this paper, based on above commonness, we propose a more general algorithm named as asynchronous COMID and prove its regret bound. We prove that asynchronous FTRL-proximal and $L2$ norm done at server are applications of asynchronous COMID, which demonstrates the convergences of above two tricks. Then, we conduct experiments to verify theoretical results. Experimental results show that compared with delayed SGD on Parameters Server, asynchronous COMID reduces the burden of the network without any harm on the mathematical convergence speed and final output.

Keywords: Asynchronous parallel · COMID · FTRL · $L2$ norm
Parameters server

1 Introduction

There are a lot of tricks in machine learning application to get higher training efficiency, better classification accuracy and the ability of solving unconvex optimization. Some of them are reasonable and well-proved, like setting a better initial model parameters to reduce training time. But most of other tricks are lack of proof. Most of those tricks can only be used suitably depending on users' experience, like deciding the size of batch and constructing a DNN. In a real situation, the majority of tricks are proved by experiments instead of rigorous mathematical proofs.

Nowadays, Parameters Server frame, based on delayed SGD algorithms, is the most popular learning frame. However, with the increasing number of workers, the burden of network would be unaffordable. Asynchronous FTRL-proximal and

© Springer Nature Singapore Pte Ltd. 2019
R. Ren et al. (Eds.): SDBA 2018, CCIS 911, pp. 55–70, 2019.
https://doi.org/10.1007/978-981-13-5910-1_6

addressing L2 norm on server are two widely used tricks to solve this problem, but they are not rigorously proved.

Above two tricks share the same commonness. They divide updating computation into two parts. One part is computed at worker. The work of this part is scanning dataset, computing the gradient of loss function without regularization term and sending this portion of loss function gradient, a sparse vector, to server. Another part is computed at server. The work of this part is computing the gradient of regularization term and updating model parameters lazily. These two parts are computed asynchronously and separately on servers and workers. Sparse data vectors in first part reduce the burden of network. Hereafter, these two tricks will be abbreviated as asynch-FTRL-proximal and L2 norm trick.

Based on above commonness, we propose and prove asynchronous Composite Objective MIrror Descent, abbr. asynch-COMID in this paper. Then, we establish the equivalence between asynchronous COMID and the above two tricks to prove above two tricks are applications of asynch-COMID. Thus, the convergences of above two tricks are also proved. We fill these gaps between application and theory of above two tricks via asynch-COMID.

1.1 Delayed SGD Algorithms and Parameters Server

SGD, Stochastic Gradient Decent, and Parallel SGD algorithms are one of the hottest topics in machine learning area [3,4,6–8,15–17,20].

SGD is designed for following minimization problems

$$\min c(w) = \frac{1}{m} \sum_{i=1}^{m} c^i(w)$$

where m stands for the amount of sample in dataset, $c^i : \ell_2 \mapsto [0, \infty]$ is convex loss function, and the vector $w \in R^d$.

Usually, $c^i(w)$ is represented by the following formula:

$$c^i(w) = r(w) + L(x^i, y^i, w \cdot x^i)$$

where $L(\cdot)$ is a convex function in $w \cdot x$, $r(w)$ is the regularized term. For example, regularized risk minimization, in this case, $r(w) = \frac{\lambda}{2} \|w\|^2$.

Delayed SGD is the most important parallel SGD algorithm. In delayed SGD algorithm, current model parameters w_t adds the gradient of older model parameters in $\tau(t)$ ($\tau(t) < t$) iterations. The iteration step for delayed SGD algorithms is:

$$w_{t+1} = w_t - \eta \partial_w c^{\tau(t)}(w_{\tau(t)})$$

where η is the learning rate or step length.

Delayed SGD algorithms first appeared in J. Langford's work [12]. In this work, the $\tau(t)$ function is fixed as Eq. 2. In Hogwild! Algorithm [10], under some restrictions, parallel SGD can be implemented in a lock-free style. Lock-free style means $\tau(t)$ can be any functions which satisfy $0 \leq t - \tau(t) \leq \tau_{max}$.

From the point of view of engineering implementation, the implement of delayed SGD is Parameters Server. Parameters Server gains high performance via the overlapping the communication time and computing time. Popular Parameters Server frame includes ps-lite in MXNET [5], TensorFlow [1], petuum [18] and so on. The method that constricts the delay was offered by Ho et al. [11].

1.2   COMID Algorithm

COMID, Composite Objective MIrror Descent, can be treat as a modified SGD. COMID does not linearize regularization term. COMID is designed for following regularized loss minimization problem [9].

$$\min c(w) = r(w) + \frac{1}{m} \sum_{i=1}^{m} L(x^i, y^i, w \cdot x^i)$$

where $r(w)$ is the convex regularization function like least squares.

The iteration step for COMID is

$$w_{t+1} = \underset{w \in \Omega}{argmin}\{\eta \langle L_t'(w_t), w - w_t \rangle + \eta r(w) + B_\psi(w, w_t)\}$$

where $B_\psi(w, w_t)$ is the Bergman Divergence

$$B_\psi(w, w_t) = \psi(w) - \psi(w_t) - \langle \nabla\psi(w_t), w - w_t \rangle$$

L_t is the abbr. of $L(x^t, y^t, w \cdot x^t)$.

In real application, the domain of w is large enough and there exist subgradients L_t', r' in $\partial f, \partial r$. All of the above conditions make every w_t satisfy the following optimality condition:

$$\eta L_t'(w_t) + \eta r'(w_{t+1}) + \nabla\psi(w_{t+1}) - \nabla\psi(w_t) = 0.$$

The diameter of the domain of w, i.e. Ω, is R, which means the domain of w is large but limited.

1.3   Asynch-COMID

In this paper, under more assumptions, we propose following asynchronous COMID iteration steps

$$w_{t+1} = \underset{w \in \Omega}{argmin}\{\eta \left\langle L_{\tau(t)}'(w_{\tau(t)}), w - w_{\tau(t)} \right\rangle$$
$$+ \eta r(w) + B_\psi(w, w_t)\} \tag{1}$$

where $\tau(t)$ is the delay function, which satisfies $0 \le t - \tau(t) \le \tau_{max}$.

To make analysis easy, in this paper, we set $\tau(t)$ as

$$\tau(t) = \begin{cases} 0 & t \le \tau_{max} \\ t - \tau_{max} & t \ge \tau_{max} \end{cases} \tag{2}$$

The optimality condition of asynch-COMID is

$$\eta L'_{\tau(t)}(w_{\tau(t)}) + \eta r'(w_{t+1}) + \nabla\psi(w_{t+1}) - \nabla\psi(w_t) = 0. \tag{3}$$

Asynch-COMID uses the delayed gradient to update the latest w.

In Parameters Server frame, the workers always push delayed information to servers. When the iteration steps contain delayed information like delayed gradient, the algorithm can run on Parameters Server frame asynchronously.

In asynch-COMID, part of gradient, $L'(\cdot)$, is delayed information. We can put this part on worker, and other part on server. What is more, the delayed information need reading sample, but scanning dataset is an exhausting job for computer. When delayed part is calculated on worker, reading dataset time can be hidden by computing and communication time. This form is suitable for the training algorithms which run on Parameters Server.

In practice, the users can divide the gradient of loss function flexibly to make transmitted data sparse. For example, when $r(w)$ contains $L1$ norm which benefits vector sparsification, it is reasonable address $L1$ norm on works.

In our work, we establish the equivalence between our asynchronous COMID and $L2$ norm tricks. Thus, we proved that addressing $L2$ norm on server would not harm algorithm convergence.

1.4 Summary

The key contributions of this paper are as follows:

1. We offer the proof of asynchronous COMID. Asynchronous COMID can work on Parameters Server frame.
2. Based on the asynchronous COMID, we prove that it is reasonable that FTRL-Proximal algorithm runs at Parameters Server frame asynchronously. We also conduct experiments to verify this theoretical result.
3. Based on the asynchronous COMID, we prove that $L2$ norm trick is reasonable. We also conduct experiments to verify this theoretical result.

In Sect. 2, we will demonstrate the proof details and theoretical results. In Sect. 3, we will present the experimental results.

2 Proof and Analysis

2.1 Notations, Setting and Assumptions

Our proof structure is based on original COMID proof [9]. Before continuing, we have to establish more notations in this subsection. The subdifferential set for the function f is denoted ∂f. $f'(w)$ is a particular subgradient in $\partial f(w)$. Subgradient is written as $\nabla f(w)$ when a function is differentiable. The inner product for u, v is $\langle u, v \rangle$ or $u \cdot v$. In this paper, we mainly deal with regularized loss function, i.e. low regret on a sequence of functions $c^t(w) = L_t(w) + r(w)$. c^t

consists of convex function r ($r > 0$) and L_t in Ω. We use the bounds of regret to guarantee the convergence. The regret is defined as

$$regret_c(T, w^*) \triangleq \sum_{t=1}^{T} [c^t(w_t) - c^t(w^*)]$$

$$= \sum_{t=1}^{T} [L_t(w_t) + r(w_t) - L_t(w^*) - r(w^*)]$$

ψ is a continuously differentiable λ-strongly convex function,

$$B_\psi(w, v) \geq \lambda/2 \left\| w - v \right\|^2 \tag{4}$$

In this paper, we also assume ψ satisfies following inequation.

$$\alpha \left\| \nabla\psi(w) - \nabla\psi(v) \right\| \geq \left\| w - v \right\| \tag{5}$$

where α is a constant.

In the proof of asynchronous algorithm, it is usual to limit the norm of gradient as following equations. We also have to obey this limit. In some works, these limitations are on whole loss function, which contain regularization part [10, 12, 21].

$$\left\| c_t(w) \right\| \leq M_{out} \tag{6}$$

almost sure for all $w \in \Omega$.

And for some work, Like Composite Objective MIrror Descent [9], the limitation is just on loss function. This limitation is presented as follows

$$\left\| L_t(w) \right\| \leq M_{in} \tag{7}$$

2.2 Asynchronous COMID

Our proof structure is based on original COMID proof [9]. We will adapt all lemmas and theorems in original COMID proof into asynch-COMID. We use the widely used limitations, i.e. Eqs. 6 and 7, to bound the "progress bound". Following lemma is the base of later proof.

Lemma 1. Under the limitation of Eqs. 4, 5, 6 and 7. For any $w \in \Omega$,

$$\eta(L_{\tau(t)}(w_{\tau(t)}) - L_{\tau(t)}(w*) + r(w_{t+1}) - r(w^*))$$
$$\leq B_\psi(w^*, w_t) - B_\psi(w^*, w_{t+1})$$
$$+ \eta^2 \alpha \tau_{max}(2M_{in}^2 + M_{in}M_{out}) \tag{8}$$

Proof. We have

$$\eta \left[L_{\tau(t)}(w_{\tau(t)}) + r(w_{t+1}) - L_{\tau(t)}(w^*) - r(w^*) \right]$$

$$\leq \eta \left[\left\langle w_{\tau(t)} - w^*, L'_{\tau(t)}(w_\tau(t)) \right\rangle \right.$$

$$\left. + \langle w_{t+1} - w^*, r'(w_{t+1}) \rangle \right]$$

$$= \eta \left[\left\langle w_{t+1} - w^*, L'_{\tau(t)}(w_\tau(t)) \right\rangle \right.$$

$$\left. + \langle w_{t+1} - w^*, r'(w_{t+1}) \rangle \right]$$

$$+ \eta \left\langle w_{\tau(t)} - w_{t+1}, L'_{\tau(t)}(w_{\tau(t)}) \right\rangle$$

Using the optimality condition, i.e. Eq. 3

$$= \left\langle w^* - w_{t+1}, \nabla\psi(w_t) - \nabla\psi(w_{t+1}) \right.$$

$$\left. - \eta L'_{\tau(t)}(w_{\tau(t)}) - \eta r'(w_{t+1}) \right\rangle$$

$$+ \langle w^* - w_{t+1}, \nabla\psi(w_{t+1}) - \nabla\psi(w_t) \rangle$$

$$+ \eta \left\langle w_{\tau(t)} - w_{t+1}, L'_{\tau(t)}(w_{\tau(t)}) \right\rangle$$

$$= B_\psi(w^*, w_t) - B_\psi(w_t, w_{t+1}) - B_\psi(w^*, w_{t+1})$$

$$+ \eta \left\langle w_{\tau(t)} - w_{t+1}, L'_{\tau(t)}(w_{\tau(t)}) \right\rangle$$

For Bregman divergences are non-negative and using Eq. 5

$$\leq B_\psi(w^*, w_t) - B_\psi(w^*, w_{t+1})$$

$$+ \eta \left\| w_{\tau(t)} - w_{t+1} \right\| \left\| L'_{\tau(t)}(w_{\tau(t)}) \right\|$$

$$\leq B_\psi(w^*, w_t) - B_\psi(w^*, w_{t+1})$$

$$+ \eta\alpha \left\| \nabla\psi(w_{\tau(t)}) - \nabla\psi(w_{t+1}) \right\| \left\| L'_{\tau(t)}(w_{\tau(t)}) \right\|$$

$$\leq B_\psi(w^*, w_t) - B_\psi(w^*, w_{t+1})$$

$$+ \eta\alpha \sum_{i=\tau(t)}^{t} \left\| \nabla\psi(w_i) - \nabla\psi(w_{i+1}) \right\| \left\| L'_{\tau(t)}(w_{\tau(t)}) \right\|$$

Using the optimality condition (Eq. 3) and lmitations (Eqs. 6 and 7)

$$\leq B_\psi(w^*, w_t) - B_\psi(w^*, w_{t+1})$$

$$+ \eta^2 \alpha \sum_{i=\tau(t)}^{t} \left\| L'_{\tau(i)}(w_{\tau(i)}) + r'(w_{i+1}) \right\| \left\| L'_{\tau(t)}(w_{\tau(t)}) \right\|$$

$$= B_\psi(w^*, w_t) - B_\psi(w^*, w_{t+1})$$

$$+ \eta^2 \alpha \sum_{i=\tau(t)}^{t} \left\| L'_{\tau(i)}(w_i) + c'(w_{i+1}) - L'_{i+1}(w_{i+1}) \right\| \cdot$$

$$\left\| L'_{\tau(t)}(w_{\tau(t)}) \right\|$$

$$\leq B_\psi(w^*, w_t) - B_\psi(w^*, w_{t+1})$$

$$+ \eta^2 \alpha (t - \tau(t))(2M_{in}^2 + M_{in}M_{out})$$

$$\leq B_\psi(w^*, w_t) - B_\psi(w^*, w_{t+1})$$

$$+ \eta^2 \alpha \tau_{max}(2M_{in}^2 + M_{in}M_{out})$$

Based on Lemma 1, following theorem shows the regret bound for the asynchronous COMID framework.

Theorem 2. Sequence w_t is the iteration point in Eq. 1. For any $w^* \in \Omega$

$$regret_c(T, w^*) \leq \frac{1}{\eta} B_\psi(w^*, w_1)$$

$$+ \sum_{i=1}^{\tau_{max}} r(w_i) + \tau_{max}\eta\alpha T(2M_{out}^2 + M_{in}M_{out}) \tag{9}$$

Proof. Lemma 1 shows

$$\eta \sum_{t=1}^{T} (L_t(w_t) - L_t(w^*) + r(w_{t+\tau}) - r(w^*)$$

$$\leq B_\psi(w^*, w_1) - B_\psi(w^*, w_{T+1})$$

$$+ \tau_{max}\eta^2\alpha T(2M_{out}^2 + M_{in}M_{out})$$

Then, we add $\sum_{i=1}^{\tau_{max}} r(w_i)$ to both sides and drop the $\sum_{i=T}^{T+\tau_{max}} r(w_i)$.

$$regret_c(T, w^*) \leq \frac{1}{\eta} B_\psi(w^*, w_1)$$

$$+ \sum_{i=1}^{\tau_{max}} r(w_i) + \tau_{max}\eta\alpha T(2M_{out}^2 + M_{in}M_{out})$$

In fact, there is no need to require what $\tau(t)$ is. It is obvious that $regret_c(T, w^*) \leq constant_1 + \eta T constant_2$, if $\tau(t)$ is a function which is almost surjective to $\mathbb{N}$ with finite elements' missing and duplication. We use Eq. 2 just because it is easy to present our main idea.

3 Application

3.1 Application 1: Asynch-FTRL-proximal

With the development of real application, the size of model parameters is extremely large and sparse. SGD is not suitable for this situation. Many sophisticated approaches, such as RDA, FOBOS and so on, do succeed in introducing sparsity. They trade off between accuracy and model parameters sparsity. COMID is one of the best trade off algorithms. FTRL-Proximal algorithm is the most popular COMID's application. FTRL-proximal is effective at producing sparse and accuracy model parameters [14].

The iteration step of FTRL-Proximal is

$$w_{t+1} = \underset{w}{argmin}((L'_{1:t} + \sum_{i=1}^{t-1} r'(w_{i+1})) \cdot w + \widetilde{\psi}_{1:t}(w) + r(w))$$

where $L'_{1:t}$ is the short hand for $\sum_{i=1}^{t} L'_t(w_t)$, ψ_t be a sequence of differentiable origin-centred convex functions ($\nabla \psi_t(0) = 0$) and $\widetilde{\psi}_t(w) = \psi_t(w - \hat{w}_t)$.

There are two versions widely used asynchronous FTRL-proximal. The first version is

$$w_{t+1} = \underset{w}{argmin}((L'_{\tau(1):\tau(t)} + \sum_{i=1}^{t-1} r'(w_{i+1})) \cdot w$$
$$+ \widetilde{\psi}_{\tau(1):\tau(t)}(w) + r(w))$$

The second one is :

$$w_{t+1} = \underset{w}{argmin}((L'_{\tau(1):\tau(t)} + \sum_{i=1}^{t-1} r'(w_{i+1})) \cdot w + \widetilde{\psi}_{1:t}(w) + r(w))$$

In this paper, we only discuss second FTRL-proximal. In following sections, asynchronous FTRL-proximal means the second version. We show equivalence between asynchronous FTRL-proximal and asynchronous COMID.

3.2 Application 2: L2 Norm Trick

$L1$, $L2$ norm is the most widely used regularization methods. $L1$ norm is mainly used to produce sparse solution. $L2$ norm, ridge regression, is the most commonly used method of regularization of ill-posed problems.

Using normal Parameters Server method, i.e. Eq. 10, workers should send the gradients to server. The $L2$ norm should be a part of loss function as theoretical analysis mentioned [10,12,21]. Just as following formulation:

$$w_{t+1} = w_t - \eta(L'(x^{\tau(t)}, y^{\tau(t)}, w \cdot x^{\tau(t)}) + \lambda w_{\tau(t)}) \tag{10}$$

Table 1. Different datasets and its sparseness

Dataset	Source	Number of features in a sample	Number of none zero features in a sample
KDD 2010(algebra)	KDD CUP 2010	20216830	20–60
Avazu	Avazu's Click-through Prediction	1,953,951	30–60
Minist8m	MNIST	780	130–200
Webspam	Webb spam corpus	16609143	70–90
KDD 2012	KDD CUP 2012	54686452	10–40

Most of the time, $L'(\cdot)$ is sparse vector. The sparsity of $L'(\cdot)$ often corresponds to the sparsity of sample vector, like the cases of linear classifier and fully connected neural network. Table 1 shows the sparsity of sample in different datasets.

However, $L2$ norm exerts great press on network for the gradient of $L2$ norm in loss function is a dense vector. Basically, gradient of $L2$ norm is the product of model parameters and a constant number. When using normal method, workers have to send a dense vector in network which would be a heavy burden for network. Especially nowadays, the number of features in sample is extremely large.

There is a trend in real application that when training a model parameters, the coders often get rid of $L2$ norm to gain high performance. But it is a trade off between training efficiency and classification accuracy. Another method to deal this problem is $L2$ norm trick. In $L2$ norm trick, $L2$ norm is done at server. The burden of network is reduced. What is more, this form is suitable for lazy updating for a lot of features would only add 0 in this form. Many Parameters Server frames use this kind of method to deal with $L2$ norm like PaddlePaddle [2], but none of them shows its reasonability. The iteration step of $L2$ norm trick is described as follows:

$$w_{t+1} = w_t - \eta(L'_{\tau(t)}(w_{\tau(t)}) + \lambda w_t)$$

3.3 Proof: Equivalence Between Asynchronous FTRL-Proximal and Asynchronous COMID

Before our proof, we introduce a lemma by H. Brendan McMahan without proof [13].

Lemma 3. Let $F : \mathbb{R}^n \mapsto \mathbb{R}$ be strongly convex with continuous partial derivatives, and let $\Phi : \mathbb{R}^n \mapsto \mathbb{R}$ be an arbitrary convex function. Define $g(x) = F(x) + \Phi(x)$. Then, there exists a unique pair $\langle x^*, \phi \rangle$ such that both

$$\phi' \in \partial\Phi(x^*)$$

and

$$x^* = \underset{x}{argmin} \, F(x) + \phi' \cdot x$$

Further, this x^* is the unique minimizer of $g(x)$.

Noting that an equivalent condition to $x^* = \underset{x}{argmin}(F(x) + \phi' \cdot x)$ is $\nabla F(x^*) + \phi' = 0$.

Lemma 3 shows that there exists a sub-gradient which satisfies

$$\underset{x}{argmin} \, F(x) + \Phi(x) = \underset{x}{argmin} \, F(x) + \phi' \cdot x. \tag{11}$$

Still, we adapt the proof of FTRL into asynchronous FTRL-proximal proof.

Following proof structure is the same as the proof in original FTRL algorithm [14].

Theorem 4. Let ψ_t be a sequence of differentiable origin-centred convex functions ($\nabla\psi_t(0) = 0$), with ψ strongly convex. Let $w_0 = \widetilde{w}_0 = 0$. For a sequence of loss functions $L_t(w) = g_t \cdot w + r(w)$, let the sequence of points $\widetilde{w}_t$ played by asynchronous COMID be

$$\hat{w}_{t+1} = \underset{w}{argmin}(L'_{\tau(t)} \cdot w + r(w) + \widetilde{B}_{1:t}(w, \hat{w}_t)) \tag{12}$$

where $\widetilde{\psi_t}(w) = \psi_t(w - \hat{w}_t)$, and $\widetilde{B}_t = B_{\widetilde{\psi}_t}$, so $\widetilde{B}_{1:t}$ is the Bregman divergence with respect to $\sum_{i=1}^{t} \widetilde{\psi}_i$. Consider the alternative sequence of point w_t played by a proximal FTRL algorithm, applied to those same L_t, defined by

$$w_{t+1} = \underset{w}{argmin}((L'_{\tau(1):\tau(t)} + \sum_{i=1}^{t-1} r'(w_{i+1})) \cdot w + \widetilde{\psi}_{1:t}(w) + r(w)) \tag{13}$$

Then, these algorithms are equivalent, in that $w_t = \hat{w}_t$ for all $t \geq 0$.

Proof. The proof is by induction. For the base case, we have $w_0 = \hat{w}_0$. From the optimality condition and Lemma 3 we know that there exists a unique $r'(w_t) \in \partial r(w_t)$

$$L'_{\tau(1):\tau(t-1)} + \sum_{i=1}^{t-2} r'(\hat{w}_{i+1}) + \nabla\widetilde{\psi}_{1:t-1}(\hat{w}_t) + r'(\hat{w}_t) = 0$$

then

$$-\nabla\widetilde{\psi}_{1:t-1}(\hat{w}_t) = L'_{\tau(1):\tau(t-1)} + \sum_{i=1}^{t-1} r'(\hat{w}_{i+1}) \tag{14}$$

Then, starting from Eq. 12

$$\hat{w}_{t+1} = \underset{w}{argmin}(L'_{\tau(t)} \cdot w + r(w) + \widetilde{B}_{1:t}(w, \hat{w}_t))$$

Using Lemma 3

$$\hat{w}_{t+1} = \underset{w}{argmin}(L'_{\tau(t)} \cdot w + r'(\hat{w}_{t+1})w + \widetilde{B}_{1:t}(w, \hat{w}_t))$$

Using the definition of $\widetilde{B}_{1:t}(w, \hat{w}_t)$

$$\hat{w}_{t+1} = \underset{w}{argmin}(L'_{\tau(t)} \cdot w + r'(\hat{w}_{t+1})w + \widetilde{B}_{1:t}(w, \hat{w}_t))$$

$$= \underset{w}{argmin}(L'_{\tau(t)} \cdot w + \widetilde{\psi}_{1:t}(w) - \widetilde{\psi}_{1:t}(\hat{w}_t)$$

$$- \nabla\widetilde{\psi}_{1:t}(\hat{w}_t)(w - w_t) + r'(\hat{w}_{t+1})w)$$

Dropping the term independent of w and $\nabla\widetilde{\psi}_t(w_t) = 0$

$$= \underset{w}{argmin}(L'_{\tau(t)} \cdot w + \widetilde{\psi}_{1:t}(w) - \nabla\widetilde{\psi}_{1:t}(\hat{w}_t)w$$

$$+ r'(\hat{w}_{t+1})w)$$

$$= \underset{w}{argmin}(L'_{\tau(t)} \cdot w + \widetilde{\psi}_{1:t}(w) - \nabla\widetilde{\psi}_{1:t-1}(\hat{w}_t)w$$

$$+ r'(\hat{w}_{t+1})w)$$

Using Eq. 14, we get

$$w_{t+1} = \underset{w}{argmin}((L'_{\tau(1):\tau(t)} + \sum_{i=1}^{t-1} r'(w_{i+1})) \cdot w + \widetilde{\psi}_{1:t}(w) + r(\hat{w}))$$

3.4 Proof: Equivalence Between Asynchronous COMID and $L2$ Norm Trick

When $r(w) = \lambda/2 \|w\|^2$, the $c_t(w) = L_t(w) + r(w)$ is the $L2$ norm regularization loss function. Here, we use λ because if the loss function is $c_t(w) = L_t(w) + \lambda/2 \|w\|^2$ and $L_t(w)$ is convex function, the $c_t(w)$ is at least λ-strongly convex function, like $L2$ norm regularization hinge loss for SVM.

Explicit asynchronous COMID algorithm with $\psi(w) = 1/2 \|w\|^2$ is as follows

$$w_{t+1} = \frac{1}{1 + \lambda\eta}w_t - \eta L_{\tau(t)}(w_{\tau(t)}) \tag{15}$$

When $\lambda\eta$ is small, using Taylor expansion, Eq. 15 is the same as

$$w_{t+1} = w_t - \eta(L_{\tau(t)}(w_{\tau(t)}) + \lambda w_t) \tag{16}$$

Comparing with Eq. 10, we can find that Eq. 16 can put their regularization term on Server when SGD algorithm runs on Parameter Server frame.

4 Numerical Experiment

4.1 Platform

Our experiments are conduced on Era supercomputer which consists of Xeon E5-2600v3 2.6G CPU connected by Infiniband.

4.2 Dataset

We use the data from Avazu's Click-through Prediction as our experiment data. Dataset is used in competition on click-through rate prediction jointly hosted by Avazu and Kaggle in 2014. We use part of the winning solution version data from Juan et al. [19], named as avazu-site.tr. Each sample in this dataset has 1000000 features.

4.3 Evaluation

For the evaluation criterion, we use the logloss of dataset instead of each sample. The logistic loss of dataset is defined as

$$logloss_{dataset} = \sum_{i=i}^{m} log(1 + exp(-1 * label * (w \cdot x)))$$

where m is the size of dataset. To clear show the gap, we will adjust the size of test dataset in different experiments. In following part, all $logloss$ is the $logloss_{dataset}$.

4.4 Implement

Our implement of above algorithms is a basic version of optimization algorithm. The batch size of all implements is 1. Our implement does not include any additional terms like bias term because our goal of following experiments is to show those tricks do not harm final output and convergence speed instead of seeking better model parameters which correspond to lower logistic loss.

4.5 Asynch-FTRL-Proximal Experiments Setting and Result

In this experiment, we will show the gaps which are between sequential FTRL-proximal algorithm and asynch-FTRL-proximal on a Parameter Server platform. The asynch-FTRL-proximal with logloss algorithm implement is described as Algorithm 1.

When the number of worker is 1, asynchronous FTRL-proximal degenerate into a sequential FTRL-proximal.

Setting. We use test dataset contain 2700 samples. We set $\lambda_1 = 0.01$ and $\lambda_2 = 0.001$. Because in this dataset, the minimum of logistic loss is close to zero, we have to adjust z_1 to let $w_1 = (1, 1, \cdots, 1)$ to have more number of epochs.

Input: Parameters α, β, λ_1, λ_2

1 **For Worker:**

2   **for** $t_1 = 1 \rightarrow$ *Forever* **do**

3   Pick Sample x_{t_1} and its label y_{t_1};

4   Pull the latest model parameters w_t from Server;

5   Calculate $p_{t_1} = sigmod(w_{t_1} \cdot x_{t_1})$;

6   Calculate $L_{t_1} = (p_{t_1} - y_{t_1})x_{t_1}$;

7   Push L_{t_1};

8   **end**

9 **For Server:**

10   Initialize z as requirement. Initialize every feature of n as 0;

11   **for** $t_2 = 1 \rightarrow$ *Forever* **do**

12   Receive $L_{\tau(t_2)}$ from one of workers;

13   Let $I \in \{i \mid$ the ith feature in $L_{\tau(t_2)} \neq 0\}$;

14   **for** $i \in I$ **do**

15   When if $|z_{t_2,i}| \leq \lambda$

16          $w_{t_2,i} = 0$;

17   Else

18          $w_{t_2,i} = -(\frac{\beta + \sqrt{n_{t_2,i}}}{\alpha} + \lambda_2)^{-1}(z_{t_2,i} - sgn(z_{t_2,i})\lambda_1)$;

19   **end**

20   **for** $i \in I$ **do**

21          $\sigma_{t_2+1,i} = \frac{1}{\alpha}(\sqrt{n_{t_2,i} + L_{\tau(t_2)}^2} - \sqrt{n_{t_2,i}})$;

22          $z_{t_2+1,i} = z_{t_2,i} + L_{\tau(t_2)} - \sigma_{t_2,i}w_{t_2,i}$;

23          $n_{t_2+1,i} = n_{t_2,i} + L_{\tau(t_2),i}^2$

24   **end**

25   **for** $i \notin I$ **do**

26   # this part does really work $\sigma_{t_2+1,i} = \sigma_{t_2,i}$;

27          $z_{t_2+1,i} = z_{t_2,i}$;

28          $n_{t_2+1,i} = n_{t_2,i}$

29   **end**

30   **end**

Algorithm 1. Per-Coordinate asynch-FTRL-Proximal with L_1 and L_2 Regularization for Logistic Regression on Parameters Server

We conduct 4 experiments in all. In each experiment, we fix the value of (α, β) and change the number of workers.

Result. Figure 1 shows the result of 4 experiments. All of those experiments prove that under different parameter setting, the convergence speed would slow with the increasing number of workers. But the gaps between different curve are small. All of those experimental results also present that asynch-FTRL-proximal does not harm final output.

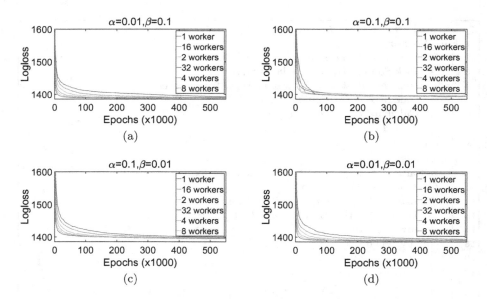

Fig. 1. The performance of asynch-FTRL-proximal with different number of worker and parameter

4.6   *L2* Trick Experiments Setting and Result

In this experiment, we will show the gaps which are between the *L2* trick and the normal method where gradient contains *L2* norm on a Parameter Server platform. Our goal is to show that above gaps are small, which means that the convergence speed of *L2* norm on server trick is closed to traditional method without any tricks.

Setting. We use test dataset contain 2500 samples. The initial value is 0 for all features in model parameters.

In impact of η experiment, we set $\lambda = 0.001$ and use 10 workers. Via different curves with various η, we can see the sensibility of *L2* norm trick for different η.

In impact of multi-workers experiment, we set $\lambda = 0.001, \eta = 0.001$. Via different curves with various number of workers, we can see the sensibility of *L2* norm trick for multi-workers.

Result. Figure 2(a) shows the performance of normal method and trick method in different η setting. With $\eta = 0.01, 0.001, 0.0001, 0.0001$, the gaps between two methods are small. Above phenomenons present that *L2* norm trick does not harm convergence speed and final output under different parameters setting.

Figure 2(b) shows the performance of normal method and trick method in different number of workers setting. As we can see, when changing the number of worker, *L2* trick does not harm convergence speed and final output.

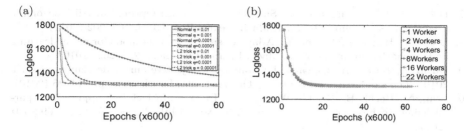

Fig. 2. (a) Impact of η: The gap between traditional method and trick method in different setting (b) Impact of multi-worker: The convergence speed of using different number of workers, with $\eta = 0.0001, \lambda = 0.001$

5 Conclusion and Future Work

In this paper, we propose and prove the convergence of asynch-COMID algorithm. Asynch-COMID reduces the burden of network via making transmitted data sparse via leaving parts of updating computation on server. We prove that two widely used tricks, $L2$ norm trick and asynch-FTRL-proximal, are applications of asynch-COMID. We also demonstrate that for certain kinds of dataset, $L2$ norm trick and asynch-FTRL-proximal exert tiny influence on convergence speed and final output.

For the future work, we will discuss more mathematical properties of asynch-COMID besides *regret*. What is more, we want to investigate the mathematical properties of dataset and loss function which determine the gap of convergence speeds and distance of the outputs from different training algorithm. It is also interesting to offer the proofs of more tricks.

Acknowledgement. This work was supported by National Natural Science Foundation of China under Grant No. 61502450, Grant No. 61432018, and Grant No. 61521092; National Key R&D Program of China under Grant No. 2016YFB0200800, Grant No. 2017YFB0202302, and Grant No. 2016YFE0100300.

References

1. Abadi, M., et al.: Tensorflow: large-scale machine learning on heterogeneous distributed systems. arXiv preprint arXiv:1603.04467 (2016)
2. Baidu: Paddlepaddle (2016). https://github.com/PaddlePaddle/Paddle
3. Bottou, L., Bousquet, O.: The tradeoffs of large scale learning. In: Conference on Neural Information Processing Systems, Vancouver, British Columbia, Canada, December, pp. 161–168 (2007)
4. Chaturapruek, S., Duchi, J.C., Re, C.: Asynchronous stochastic convex optimization: the noise is in the noise and SGD don't care, pp. 1531–1539 (2015)
5. Chen, T., et al.: Mxnet: a flexible and efficient machine learning library for heterogeneous distributed systems. Statistics (2015)
6. Dean, J., et al.: Large scale distributed deep networks. In: International Conference on Neural Information Processing Systems, pp. 1223–1231 (2012)

7. Dekel, O., Gilad-Bachrach, R., Shamir, O., Xiao, L.: Optimal distributed online prediction using mini-batches. J. Mach. Learn. Res. **13**(1), 165–202 (2012)
8. Duchi, J., Hazan, E., Singer, Y.: Adaptive subgradient methods for online learning and stochastic optimization. J. Mach. Learn. Res. **12**(7), 257–269 (2010)
9. Duchi, J., Tewari, A., Chicago, T.: Composite objective mirror descent. In: COLT 2010 - The Conference on Learning Theory, Haifa, Israel, June, pp. 14–26 (2010)
10. Feng, N., Recht, B., Re, C., Wright, S.J.: Hogwild!: a lock-free approach to parallelizing stochastic gradient descent. Adv. Neural Inf. Process. Syst. **24**, 693–701 (2011)
11. Ho, Q., et al.: More effective distributed ml via a stale synchronous parallel parameter server. Adv. Neural Inf. Process. Syst. **2013**(2013), 1223–1231 (2013)
12. Langford, J., Smola, A.J., Zinkevich, M.: Slow learners are fast. In: Advances in Neural Information Processing Systems 22: Conference on Neural Information Processing Systems 2009. Proceedings of A Meeting Held 7–10 December 2009, Vancouver, British Columbia, Canada, pp. 2331–2339 (2009)
13. Mcmahan, H.B.: Follow-the-regularized-leader and mirror descent: equivalence theorems and l1 regularization. JMLR **15**, 2011 (2013)
14. Mcmahan, H.B., et al.: Ad clickprediction: a view from the trenches. In: ACM SIGKDD International Conference on Knowledge Discovery and Data Mining, pp. 1222–1230 (2013)
15. Nemirovski, A., Juditsky, A., Lan, G., Shapiro, A.: Robust stochastic approximation approach to stochastic programming. Siam J. Optim. **19**, 1574–1609 (2009)
16. Nesterov, Y.: Primal-dual subgradient methods for convex problems. Math. Program. **120**(1), 221–259 (2009)
17. Shalev-Shwartz, S., Srebro, N.: SVM optimization: inverse dependence on training set size. In: International Conference on Machine Learning, pp. 928–935 (2008)
18. Xing, E.P., et al.: Petuum: a new platform for distributed machine learning on big data. IEEE Trans. Big Data **1**(2), 49–67 (2013)
19. Yu, H., Lo, H., Hsieh, H.: Feature engineering and classifier ensemble for KDD cup 2010. In: JMLR Workshop and Conference (2010)
20. Zhu, Y., Chatterjee, S., Duchi, J.C., Lafferty, J.D.: Local minimax complexity of stochastic convex optimization. In: Neural Information Processing Systems, pp. 3423–3431 (2016)
21. Zinkevich, M., Weimer, M., Smola, A.J., Li, L.: Parallelized stochastic gradient descent. Adv. Neural Inf. Process. Syst. **23**(23), 2595–2603 (2010)

Algorithms

A Parallel Solving Algorithm on GPU for the Time-Domain Linear System with Diagonal Sparse Matrices

Yifei Xia[1], Jiaquan Gao[1,2(✉)], and Guixia He[2]

[1] School of Computer Science and Technology,
Nanjing Normal University, Nanjing 210023, China
`springf12@163.com`
[2] Zhijiang College, Zhejiang University of Technology, Hangzhou 310024, China
`hegx_1022@163.com`

Abstract. For the time-domain linear system with diagonal sparse matrices, based on the popular preconditioned generalized minimum residual method (GMRES), we proposed an efficient solving algorithm on the graphics processing unit (GPU), which is called T-GMRES. In the proposed T-GMRES, three are the following novelties: (1) a new sparse storage format BRCSD is presented to alleviate the drawback of the diagonal format (DIA) that a large number of zeros are filled to maintain the diagonal structure when many diagonals are far away from the main diagonal; (2) an efficient sparse matrix-vector multiplication on GPU for BRCSD is proposed; and (3) for assembling the sparse matrix for BRCSD and the vector efficiently on GPU, a new kernel is suggested. The experimental results have validated the high efficiency and good performance of our proposed algorithm.

Keywords: Linear system · Diagonal sparse matrices
Parallel solving algorithm · CUDA · GPU

1 Introduction

For many problems in various fields such as computational fluid dynamics and electromagnetics, after the partial differential equations (PDEs) that describe the evolutions of them are discretized by the popular numerical methods such as the finite difference method (FDM), finite volume method (FVM), and structure-preserving algorithm (SPA) [1], the discrete PDEs can usually be formulated as the following time-domain linear system:

$$A^n u^{n+1} = b^n. \tag{1}$$

The research has been supported by the Natural Science Foundation of Zhejiang Province, China under grant number LY17F020021, and the Natural Science Foundation of Jiangsu Province, China under grant number BK20171480, and the Open Project Program of the State Laboratory of Computer Architecture under grant number CARCH201603, and the Qing Lan Project of Nanjing Normal University.

© Springer Nature Singapore Pte Ltd. 2019
R. Ren et al. (Eds.): SDBA 2018, CCIS 911, pp. 73–84, 2019.
https://doi.org/10.1007/978-981-13-5910-1_7

Here A^n that depends on u^n is a diagonal sparse matrix at each time step t_n, and has the same sparse structure for different time step t_n; u^{n+1} is the unknown solution; and b^n depends on u^n at each time step t_n.

Given that graphics processing units (GPUs) have drawn much attention and have become increasingly strong competitors among the general-purpose parallel programming systems over recent years [2], we attempt to develop the suitable and flexible parallel algorithm on GPU for solving such a time-domain linear system in this paper. Obviously, two main problems need to be solved: (1) assembling A^n and b^n quickly on GPU at each time step t_n, and (2) designing an efficient GPU-accelerated parallel algorithm to solve the linear system with the diagonal sparse matrix at each time step t_n.

If A^n and b^n are calculated on the CPU, u^n need to be transferred from GPU to CPU and they need to be transferred from CPU to GPU after A^n and b^n are calculated at each time step t_n. In order to avoid the overhead of transmission, we present an efficient parallel algorithm to assemble A^n and b^n on GPU. Each row in A^n or each element in b^n is assigned to a thread. As we know, the generalized minimum residual method (GMRES) [4] is one of the most popular iterative methods for solving such a linear system (1) at each time step t_n. And researchers have recently developed a great number of GMRES algorithms on the GPU architecture for large-sized sparse linear systems [5–8]. Thus, based on a GEMRES version [8], we propose an efficient GPU-accelerated algorithm for solving the time-domain linear system with diagonal sparse matrices at each time step t_n.

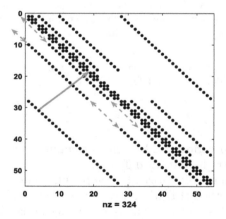

Fig. 1. A DIA sample

The main components of GMRES include the sparse matrix-vector multiplication (SpMV), vector operation (excluding inner product), inner product, and dense matrix-vector multiplication. Given a great deal of cost of SpMV in GMRES, most researchers focus on accelerating the implementation of SpMV on

GPU. Based on the compute unified device architecture (CUDA), some efficient SpMV kernels are proposed for well-known sparse matrix storage formats such as CSR, DIA, ELL (ELLPACK/ITPACK), COO, and HYB [3]. Thus, many new efficient SpMV kernels have also been proposed for GPUs using the variants of the CSR, ELL, and COO storage formats [9–12]. The overview of efficient storage formats and their corresponding SpMV kernels can be found in [13]. Each storage format has its ideal matrix type [3, 14, 15]. DIA is the most appropriate storage format for the diagonal sparse matrix. All non-zeros on the same diagonal share the same index. However, a large number of zeros should be filled to maintain the diagonal structure, when the diagonals are broken by long zero sections or many diagonals are far away from the main diagonal, as shown in Fig. 1. This may reduce the performance since the filled zeros consume extra computation and memory resources [16].

In this paper, we focus on this case where a lot of diagonals are far away from the main diagonal. We propose a new sparse storage format BRCSD. Different from existing work [3, 16], we divide the matrix into pieces according to the row while trying to keep each piece with less filling, and then each row piece is stored according to DIA. Furthermore, a new SpMV kernel for BRCSD are presented. Finally, on the basis of the proposed kernels, we present an efficient parallel solving algorithm on GPU for the linear system with diagonal sparse matrices. Experimental results show that the BRCSD SpMV kernel is better than the popular CSR and DIA SpMV kernels, the kernel for assembling the matrix and vector is valid, and the proposed parallel solving algorithm on GPU for the time-domain linear system with diagonal sparse matrices is efficient and has high parallelism.

The remainder of this paper is organized as follows. In the second section, the parallel solving algorithm for the time-domain linear system with diagonal sparse matrices is proposed. Experimental results are given in the third section. The fourth section contains our conclusions and points to our future research directions.

2   GPU Implementation

Based on GMRES in [8], here we present a parallel solving algorithm on GPU for solving the time-domain linear system in Eq. (1). We call our proposed algorithm T-GMRES. The parallel framework of T-GMRES is shown in Fig. 2.

2.1   BRCSD Format

DIA is formed by two arrays: **data**, which stores the nonzero values, and **offsets**, which stores the offset of each diagonal from the main diagonal [3]. E.g., the diagonal sparse matrix shown in Fig. 3 is stored as

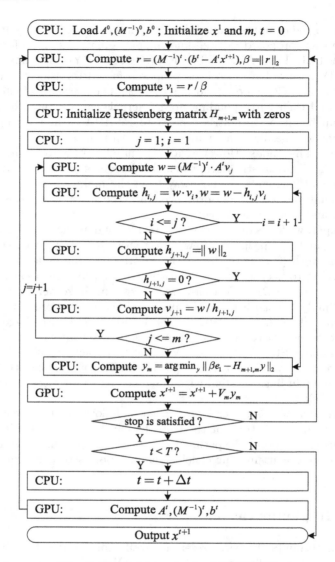

Fig. 2. Parallel framework of T-GMRES

$$\mathbf{data} = \begin{bmatrix} 0 & 1 & 2 & 3 \\ 0 & 4 & 5 & 6 \\ 7 & 8 & 9 & 0 \\ 10 & 11 & 12 & 0 \\ 13 & 14 & 15 & 0 \\ 16 & 17 & 0 & 0 \end{bmatrix}, \text{ and } \mathbf{offsets} = [-2, 0, 1, 4].$$

$$\mathbf{data} = \begin{bmatrix} 0 & 1 & 2 & 3 \\ 0 & 4 & 5 & 6 \\ 7 & 8 & 9 & 0 \\ 10 & 11 & 12 & 0 \\ 13 & 14 & 15 & 0 \\ 16 & 17 & 0 & 0 \end{bmatrix}, \text{ and } \mathbf{offsets} = [-2, 0, 1, 4].$$

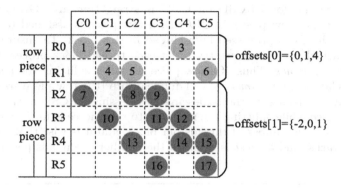

Fig. 3. An example of diagonal sparse matrix

We observe that the zero values are filled into **data** because of the offset of diagonals. The greater the offset is, the more the zero values are filled. To alleviate this drawback of DIA, we present a new sparse storage format BRCSD. First, we divide the matrix into pieces according to the row, and try to keep each piece with less filling. E.g., the matrix shown in Fig. 3 can be divided into two pieces. Second, we represent the matrix as follows:

$$\text{matrix} = \{\text{offsets}[0], \text{offsets}[1], \dots, \text{offsets}[n]\}, \tag{2}$$

where offsets[i] is the offset of each diagonal from the main diagonal in the ith piece. E.g., the matrix shown in Fig. 3 is represented as follows:

$$\text{matrix} = \{[0, 1, 4], [-2, 0, 1]\}.$$

Finally, we represent the matrix by the following two arrays:

$$\mathbf{brcsd\_offsets} = \{r_0 | \text{offsets}[0], r_1 | \text{offsets}[1], \dots, r_n | \text{offsets}[n]\},$$
$$\mathbf{brcsd\_data} = \{\text{data}[0], \text{data}[1], \dots, \text{data}[n]\}.$$

Here r_i is the starting row number of the ith row piece. E.g., the matrix shown in Fig. 3 is represented as follows:

$$\textbf{brcsd\_offsets} = \{0|[0,1,4],2|[-2,0,1]\},$$
$$\textbf{brcsd\_data} = \{[1,4,2,5,3,6],$$
$$[7,10,13,16,8,11,14,17,9,12,15,0]\}.$$

2.2 Sparse Matrix-Vector Multiplication

Parallelizing SpMV for BRCSD on GPU is straightforward. Given that the matrix is split into row pieces in BRCSD, a row piece is assigned to a thread block, and each row is processed by a thread in this block. To ensure the load balance of each thread block, we try to let each thread block process the same number of rows, *nrows*. Thus, if a row piece size after splitting the matrix into row pieces is larger than *nrows*, we will divide it into ⌈the row piece size/*nrows*⌉ row pieces again. To assure the coalescing of accessing BRCSD arrays, the size of each row piece while splitting the matrix into row pieces is finely modified to be a multiple of the number of threads per block, and it is wise that *nrows* is a multiple of warps, and at best is equal to the number of threads per block.

```
Input: brcsd_data, u
Output: y
01: block_id ← blockIdx.x;
02: local_id ← threadIdx.x;
03: offsets_id=block_id<1?0:1;
04: switch( offsets_id ){
05:   case 0: //for offsets[0]=[0,1,4]
06:     tmp←0.0;
07:     tmp+=brcsd_data[block_id· 2+local_id] ·u[local_id+block_id ·2];
08:     tmp+=brcsd_data[2+block_id· 2+local_id] ·u[1+local_id+block_id ·2];
09:     y[local_id]←tmp;
10:     break;
11:   case 1: //for offsets[1]=[-2,0,1]
12:     tmp←0.0;
13:     tmp+=brcsd_data[6+block_id· 2-2+local_id] ·u[-2+local_id+block_id ·2];
14:     tmp+=brcsd_data[6+4+block_id· 2-2+local_id] ·u[0+local_id+block_id ·2];
15:     tmp+=brcsd_data[6+8+block_id· 2-2+local_id] ·u[1+local_id+block_id ·2];
16:     y[block_id ·2+local_id]←tmp;
17:     break;
18: }
```

Fig. 4. SpMV kernel for BRCSD on GPU

In the following, we generate the SpMV kernel. First, we get the thread block ID *block_id* = *blockIdx.x*, the local thread ID *local_id* = *threadIdx.x*, and identify which offset array the thread block processes. Because a thread block deals with a row piece, block $block\_id$ processes the ith offset array only if satisfying the following condition:

$$r_i/nrows \leqslant block\_id < r_{i+1}/nrows.$$

Next, we generate the SpMV operations for block $block\_id$ with the ith offset array. For local thread $local\_id$, when processing the jth diagonal, the location of nonzero is $\sum_{z=1}^{i}(r_z - r_{z-1}) \times$ offsets$[z\text{-}1].length + (r_{i+1} - r_i) \times j + (block\_id \times nrows - r_i) + local\_id$, and its corresponding location in vector u is $block\_id \times nrows + local\_id+$ offsets$[i].j$.

Finally, accumulating the product of all diagonals in the ith offset array, we store it to y at location $block\_id \times nrows + local\_id$.

E.g., for the matrix in Fig. 3, letting $nrows = 2$, we show the main procedure of SpMV kernel for BRCSD on GPU in Fig. 4.

2.3   Assemble the Matrix and Vector

For assembling A^n for BRCSD efficiently at each time step t_n on GPU, we present a new kernel. In the proposed kernel, a row piece is assigned to a thread block, and a thread assembles a row in this block. Next, let us introduce the procedure.

First, similar to SpMV kernel, we get the thread block ID $block\_id = blockIdx.x$, the local thread ID $local\_id = threadIdx.x$, and identify which offset array the thread block processes. Second, we generate the kernel operations for thread block $block\_id$ with the ith offset array. For local thread $local\_id$, when processing the jth diagonal, the location of the nonzero item that needs to be calculated is $\sum_{z=1}^{i}(r_z - r_{z-1}) \times$ offsets$[z\text{-}1].length + (r_{i+1} - r_i) \times j + (block\_id \times nrows - r_i) + local\_id$, and thus the value in this location can be computed through the known formula.

Assembling b^n at each time step t_n on GPU is straightforward, each thread computes an elemental value through the known formula. In order to reduce the number of kernels, the two kernels of assembling A^n and b^n are grouped into a kernel, which is called AssemblingMV.

2.4   Vector Operation and Inner Product

For T-GMRES, the vector-operation and inner-product kernels are needed. Although CUBLAS [17] has shown good performance for the vector operation and the inner product of vector, the use of CUBLAS does not allow to group several operations into a single kernel. Here in order to optimize these operations, we try to group several operations into a single kernel. Therefore, we adopt the idea of constructing the vector-operation and inner-product decision trees that are suggested in [8]. Utilizing the vector-operation and inner-product decision trees, the optimal vector-operation and inner-product kernels and their corresponding CUDA parameters can be obtained. For readers that are interested in this work, please refer to the publication [8].

2.5 Preconditioner and Other

For improving the convergence of T-GMRES, the preconditioned technique is adopted. For the sake of simplicity, we choose M^n as the A^n diagonal at each time step t_n, which is straightforward to inverse and provides a relatively good preconditioning, in so far as the matrices are not too ill-conditioned.

To solve the least-squares problem, it is kept running serially on the CPU because its operation is negligible when m is a small number. For the dense matrix-vector multiplication on GPU, we use the GEMV-Adaptive algorithm that are proposed by He et al. [18] because it has higher performance than that of CUBLAS [17] and KBLAS [19].

3 Experimental Results

In this section, we test the validity of our proposed T-GMRES. The experimental environments include one machine which is equipped with an Intel Xeon Quad-Core CPU and an NVIDIA GTX1070 GPU and another machine with an Intel Xeon Quad-Core CPU and an NVIDIA Tesla K40c. Our source codes are compiled and executed using the CUDA toolkit 9.0 [2]. The test matrices come from the University of Florida Sparse Matrix Collection [20] and other publications [8,22]. Table 1 summarizes the information of the test matrices, including the dimension, number of diagonals, and total number of nonzeros.

Table 1. Descriptions of test matrices

Matrix	Dimension	Diagonals	Nonzeros
cage09	$2,097,152 \times 2,097,152$	6	$4,718,592$
cage10	$4,194,304 \times 4,194,304$	6	$9,437,184$
troso1	$1,228,800 \times 1,228,800$	9	$3,778,542$
troso2	$4,915,200 \times 4,915,200$	9	$14,929,902$
G9	$1,500,000 \times 1,500,000$	12	$10,499,990$
nlpkkt200	$8,388,480 \times 8,388,480$	23	$18,869,888$
rgg_n_2_20	$1,638,400 \times 1,638,400$	41	$2,580,474$
rgg_n_2_23	$8,192,000 \times 8,192,000$	41	$5,222,394$
3DKGS	$1,769,472 \times 1,769,472$	9	$14,045,184$
2DKGS	$2,097,152 \times 2,097,152$	7	$12,574,720$
2DMaxwell512	$786,432 \times 786,432$	18	$5,898,222$
2DMaxwell1024	$3,145,728 \times 3,145,728$	18	$23,592,942$

First, we test the validity of our proposed BRCSD SpMV kernel by comparing it with CSR and DIA SpMV kernels [3]. The main reasons of choosing the two kernels are that DIA is the most appropriate for diagonal sparse matrices, and

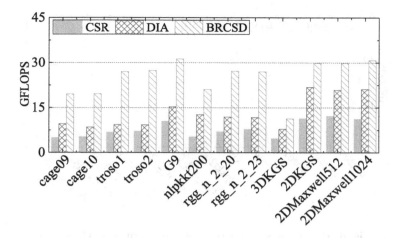

Fig. 5. Performance comparison of three kernels on K40c

BRCSD is based on row pieces. Figures 5 and 6 show the performance comparison of three kernels on K40c and GTX1070 GPUs, respectively. GFLOPS values are calculated on the basis of the assumption of two flops per nonzero entry for a matrix [3,21]. We observe that BRCSD is advantageous over CSR and DIA for all matrices on two GPUs. Compared to CSR, BRCSD on k40c and GTX1070 achieves average performance improvement of 88.46% and 31.93%, respectively. The average performance improvement of BRCSD vs DIA on k40c and GTX1070 is 219.63% and 137.58%, respectively.

Second, we take GTX1070 to test the validity of AssemblingMV. The test matrices are the coefficient matrices of the time-domain linear systems at one time step, which are obtained by using SPA to discretize the two/three-dimensional Klein-Gordon-Schrödinger equation (KGS) with six grids [22], as shown in Table 2. The second column is the size of grids. E.g., 512^2 denotes the two-dimensional grid 512×512 and 96^3 denotes the three-dimensional grid $96 \times 96 \times 96$. The third and fourth columns show the rows and nonzeros of matrices, respectively. The execution time of assembling matrices on the CPU and the GPU is shown in the fifth and sixth columns, respectively. The seventh column is the speedup of CPU vs GPU. We observe that the speedup ranges from 129.03 to 144.73 and the average speedup is 135.88. This verifies the validity of our proposed AssemblingMV.

Finally, we take GTX1070 to test the performance of T-GMRES by comparing it with its corresponding serial implementation on the CPU. The time-domain linear system is obtained by using SPA to discretize the three-dimensional Klein-Gordon-Schrödinger equation with the grid $96 \times 96 \times 96$ [22]. The test time T is set as 0.1, 0.2, 0.3, . . . , 1.5 in order. For each time T, the time step Δt is 0.01, all algorithms stop when the maximum iteration exceeds 40 at each time step, and a restarting limit $m = 20$. Figure 7 shows the execution time comparison of two algorithms with T changes from 0.1 to 1.5. Our proposed

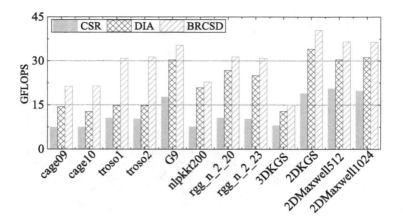

Fig. 6. Performance comparison of three kernels on GTX1070

Table 2. Execution time of AssemblingMV

Seq	Grids	Rows	Nonzeros	CPU	GPU	$\frac{CPU}{GPU}$
1	512^2	524,288	3,141,632	43.87	0.34	129.03
2	640^2	819,200	4,910,080	69.70	0.53	131.51
3	1024^2	2,097,152	12,574,720	176.56	1.33	132.75
4	96^3	1,769,472	14,045,184	163.55	1.13	144.73
5	128^3	4,194,304	33,357,824	377.62	2.71	139.34
6	192^3	7,529,536	112,803,840	1266.21	9.18	137.93

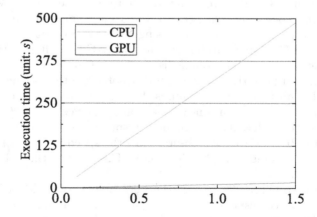

Fig. 7. Execute time of two algorithms as T changes.

T-GMRES has almost 35 times faster than its corresponding serial implementation on the CPU by observing Fig. 7.

From the above observations, we can conclude that our proposed BRCSD SpMV kernel and AssemblingMV are efficient, and T-GMRES has high parallelism and is efficient in solving the time-domain linear system with diagonal sparse matrices.

4   Conclusion

In this paper, we present an efficient algorithm on GPU, T-GMRES, for solving the time-domain linear system with diagonal sparse matrices. Experimental results show that our proposed T-GMRES is efficient and has high parallelism. Next, we will further do research in this field, and apply the proposed solving algorithm to the real problems.

References

1. Qin, M., Wang, Y.: Structure-Preserving Algorithm of Partial Differential Equations. Zhejiang Science and Technology Press, Hangzhou (2011)
2. CUDA C Programming Guide 9.0. http://docs.nvidia.com/cuda/cuda-c-programming-guide
3. Bell, N., Garland, M.: Implementing sparse matrix-vector multiplication on throughput-oriented processors. In: Proceedings Conference on High Performance Computing Networking, Storage and Analysis (SC 2009), pp. 14–19. ACM, New York (2009)
4. Saad, Y.: Iterative Methods for Sparse Linear Systems, second version. SIAM, Philadelphia, PA (2003)
5. Couturier, R., Domas, S.: Sparse systems solving on GPUs with GMRES. J. Supercomput. **59**(3), 1504–1516 (2012)
6. Li, R., Saad, Y.: GPU-accelerated preconditioned iterative linear solvers. J. Supercomput. **63**(2), 443–466 (2013)
7. Yang, B., Liu, H., Chen, Z.: Preconditioned GMRES solver on multiple-GPU architecture. Comput. Math. Appl. **72**(4), 1076–1095 (2016)
8. Gao, J., Wu, K., Wang, Y., Qi, P., He, G.: GPU-accelerated preconditioned GMRES method for two-dimensional Maxwell's equations. Int. J. Comput. Math. **94**(10), 2122–2144 (2017)
9. Choi, J.W., Singh, A., Vuduc, R.W.: Model-driven autotuning of sparse matrix-vector multiply on GPUs. In: Proceedings of the 15th ACM SIGPLAN Symposium Principles and Practice of Parallel Programming (PPoPP 2010), pp. 9–14. ACM, Bangalore (2010)
10. Yan, S., Li, C., Zhang, Y.: yaSpMV: Yet another SpMV framework on GPUs. In: Proceedings of the 19th ACM SIGPLAN Symposium Principles and Practice of Parallel Programming (PPoPP 2014), pp. 107–118. ACM, New York (2014)
11. Kreutzer, M., Hager, G., Wellein, G.: A unified sparse matrix data format for efficient general sparse matrix-vector multiply on modern processors with wide simd units. SIAM J. Sci. Comput. **36**(5), C401–C423 (2014)
12. Gao, J., Liang, R., Wang, J.: Research on the conjugate gradient algorithm with a modified incomplete Cholesky preconditioner on GPU. J. Parallel Distr. Comput. **74**(2), 2088–2098 (2014)

13. Filippone, S., Cardellini, V., Barbieri, D.: Sparse matrix-vector multiplication on GPGPUs. ACM Trans. Math. Software **43**(4), 30 (2017)
14. Gao, J., Wang, Y., Wang, J.: A novel multi-graphics processing unit parallel optimization framework for the sparse matrix-vector multiplication. Concurr. Comput.-Pract. E. **29**(5), e3936 (2017)
15. Gao, J., Wang, Y., Wang, J., Liang, R.: Adaptive optimization modeling of preconditioned conjugate gradient on multi-GPUs. ACM Trans. Parallel Comput. **3**(3), 16 (2016)
16. Sun, X., Zhang, Y., Wang, T.: Optimizing SpMV for diagonal sparse matrices on GPU. In: 2011 International Conference on Parallel Processing, ICPP 2011, pp. 492–501. IEEE, Taipei (2011)
17. CUBLAS Library 9.0. http://docs.nvidia.com/cuda/cublas
18. He, G., Gao, J., Wang, J.: Efficient dense matrix-vector multiplication on GPU. Concurr. Comput.-Pract. E., e4705(2018). https://doi.org/10.1002/cpe.4705
19. Abdelfattah, A., Keyes, D., Ltaief, H.: KBLAS: an optimized library for dense matrix-vector multiplication on GPU accelerators. ACM Trans. Math. Software **42**(3), 18 (2014)
20. Davis, T.A., Hu, Y.: The university of florida sparse matrix collection. ACM Trans. Math. Software **38**(1), 1–25 (2011)
21. Gao, J., Zhou, Y., He, G., Xia, Y.: A multi-GPU parallel optimization model for the preconditioned conjugate gradient algorithm. Parallel Comput. **63**, 1–16 (2017)
22. Wang, T., Zhao, X., Jiang, J.: Unconditional and optimal H^2-error estimates of two linear and conservative finite difference schemes for the Klein-Gordon-Schrödinger equation in high dimensions. Adv. Comput. Math. **44**(2), 477–503 (2018)

An Unsupervised Anomaly Detection Algorithm for Time Series Big Data

Wenqing Wang, Junpeng Bao[⊠], and Hui He

Xi'an Jiaotong University, Xi'an 710049, People's Republic of China
baojp@mail.xjtu.edu.cn

Abstract. Many time series anomaly detection algorithms are hard to be applied in real scenarios for two reasons. Firstly some of them are supervised since training data is required to define the normal behavior, but it is expensive to annotate the normal part for large volume data. Secondly, many algorithms are parameter-laden, which are hard to be generalized to different dataset. This paper is motivated to overcome these disadvantages. It is believed that a normal behavior is a subsequence which is similar to some subsequences in a time series while an anomaly is a subsequence which is distinct from the others. In order to improve the efficiency of searching anomaly, we first select candidate anomalies rather than check all subsequences. We roughly distinguish the candidate anomalies from normal subsequences by transforming each subsequence into a string. If a string corresponds to only one subsequence, then it is a candidate anomaly. And the subsequences of the same string represent a kind of normal behavior. Secondly, similarity threshold is calculated according to the similarity between normal behaviors. If the similarity between a candidate anomaly and its nearest neighbor is lower than the threshold, then this candidate is determined to be anomalous. We conduct extensive experiments on benchmark datasets from diverse domains and compare our method with the state-of-the-art method. The empirical results show that our method can reach high detection rate in an unsupervised and parameter-lite manner.

Keywords: Unsupervised anomaly detection · Parameter-lite
Real-valued time series

1 Introduction

Time series anomaly detection has been studied for decades because of its wide application such as intrusion detection, event detection, system diagnosis, disease surveillance and so on. However many anomaly detection algorithms are difficult to use for two reasons. Firstly, many of them [2, 4, 7, 12] are supervised, which require the samples of normal behavior. However, it is expensive or even impossible to obtain all kinds of normal behaviors for big data. Secondly, some algorithms [2, 6, 11] have many non-intuitive parameters, which is hard to achieve good results on different datasets. Just as Keogh points out parameter-laden algorithms can achieve excellent performance on one dataset by tuning parameters but fail to generalize to new datasets [5]. Indeed, this work is motivated by getting rid of or alleviating the above problem. We are aiming for an algorithm more easy and friendly to use.

© Springer Nature Singapore Pte Ltd. 2019
R. Ren et al. (Eds.): SDBA 2018, CCIS 911, pp. 85–94, 2019.
https://doi.org/10.1007/978-981-13-5910-1_8

In this paper, an anomaly is defined as a distinct subsequence in a time series, which is not similar to any others. A straightforward idea to find such kind of subsequence is to compare the similarity between each subsequence and the others. If the maximum similarity between one subsequence and the others is smaller than a threshold, it is anomalous. This leaves two questions. The first is about time efficiency. It is time consuming of pairwise similarity calculation since the time complexity is $O(n^2)$ where n is the number of subsequences. In order to solve this problem, we first reduce the anomaly searching space. Specifically, candidate anomalies are distinguished from the whole time series by discretization. Each subsequence is transformed into a string. If a string corresponds to only one subsequence, this subsequence is a potential anomaly. Then our method calculates the similarity between each candidate anomaly and the other subsequences. The time complexity is $O(mn)$ where m is the number of candidate anomalies and n is the number of remainder subsequences, m<<n.

The other question is how to compute the similarity threshold adaptively. Obviously, the similarity between an anomaly and the other subsequences is lower than the average similarity between normal behaviors. Thus the average similarity between normal behaviors is selected to be a threshold. Normal behavior can be obtained by the previous discretization step. If some subsequences are projected to the same string after transformation, they are similar and represent one normal pattern. Therefore, in our method, a normal behavior does not need to be manually labeled which implies our algorithm is unsupervised.

The similarity measure is an essential step for a machine learning algorithm. For some normal subsequences in a time series with trend, which are similar with others in shape but different in amplitude, it will be considered to be different with others by using Euclidian distance so as to make false alarm. We employ Pearson correlation coefficient to deal with such problem, which will be discussed in Sect. 3 in details. In our method, subsequence length is the only parameter need to be specified. For most datasets, our method is not sensitive to the variation of subsequence length.

The rest of paper is organized as follows. Section 2 is about related work. Section 3 introduces our method in detail. In Sect. 4, we compare our method with a state-of-the-art method in terms of anomaly detection rate and analyze the parameter sensitivity in our method. Section 5 provides conclusions.

2   Related Work

There are many literatures about time series anomaly detection methods. One class is prediction based methods [7–9], which consider an anomaly as a point with great difference between its observed and predicted value. Prediction techniques are various including LSTM [7], exponential model [8], support vector regression [6] and so on. Another common idea for anomaly detection is clustering based methods [13, 14]. Subsequences within small or sparse clusters are considered as anomalies. In addition, similarity based methods [1, 2, 10, 15] are effective for anomaly detection, which is reported to be more simple and robust as compared to model-based, cluster-based methods in [15].

Keogh et al. [1] proposed the most unusual discord discovery algorithm, which could be used as anomaly detector. It is reported that their optimized brute force algorithm is 3 to 4 times faster than the pure brute force algorithm by taking advantage of heuristic ordered search. However, if we want to find the top K discords, this pruning strategy will be weakened since the rank of each subsequence is needed. In anomaly detection problem, there are often several discords and the number of discords is also unknown. In this case, time efficiency and accuracy of the optimized brute force algorithm will decrease.

Jones et al. [2] proposed the SST (Statistical and Smoothed Trajectory) exemplar based method to detect anomaly in one dimensional real-valued time series. In their work, an anomaly is defined as the subsequence in a test time series which does not appear in a training time series. In their algorithms, statistical and smoothed trajectory features are used to represent each subsequence. And hierarchical clustering of SST features is employed to learn exemplars from a training time series. Each exemplar represents a set of similar feature, which corresponds to a motif in a training time series. Then the anomaly score of each subsequence in a test time series is measured by the Euclidean distance with its nearest exemplar. The empirical results show that SST algorithm outperforms the algorithm proposed by Keogh [1] in terms of both accuracy and speed. In particular, there is a prominent speed improvement over 20,000 when it handles a large time series with 11 million time steps. Thus we consider SST exemplar as the state-of-the-art algorithm and compare our method with it in Sect. 4. But it has some disadvantages: (1) it must have a training time series, which defines normal behavior and does not contain any anomaly. However, it is expensive to manually split a time series into training and testing time series. (2) SST exemplar algorithm is parameter-laden, which includes 5 parameters. Therefore it is hard for user to tune parameters to achieve a good result.

3   The Proposed Method

3.1   Basic Idea

Definition 1. Subsequence: given a time series $T = [t_0, t_1, \ldots t_{n-1}]$ with n time steps, a subsequence T_i with length m is defined as $T_i = [t_i, t_{i+1}, \ldots t_j, \ldots t_{m+i-1}]$, where i is start point and $i <= j <= m + i - 1, j <= n$.

Definition 2. Anomalous subsequence: for a subsequence T_i, if $\max\{sim(T_i, T_j)\} < \delta$, then T_i is an anomalous subsequence, where T_j is a non-self subsequence of T_i and $sim(.)$ is a similarity measure. δ is the similarity threshold.

Definition 3. Non-self subsequence: for a subsequence T_i with length m, if a subsequence T_j satisfies $j >= i + m$ or $j <= i - m$, i.e. they are non-overlapping, then T_j is a non-self subsequence of T_i.
The anomaly score of each subsequence T_i is the similarity between T_i and its nearest neighbor, which is denoted as $Sim_{1NN}(T_i)$. If $Sim_{1NN}(T_i)$ is very small, then T_i is very likely to be an anomaly. However, the time complexity of this process is $O(n^2)$ where n is the number of subsequence.

In order to address this problem, anomaly candidates are firstly selected and we only need to calculate the similarity between anomaly candidates and their non-self subsequences. To further reduce the pairwise similarity computation, we employ a threshold δ. For an anomalous subsequence T_i, which is distinct from all the others, thus $sim(T_i, T_j) < \delta$ is satisfied for any non-self subsequences T_j. On the contrary, for a normal subsequence T_i, there exists some non-self subsequences T_j satisfying $sim(T_i, T_j) > = \delta$.

According to this principle, we perform an early abandoning strategy to compare a subsequence and its non-self subsequences. For subsequence T_i, if the similarity between T_i and its current non-self subsequence T_j is greater than δ, then T_i must be a normal subsequence and there is no need to compute the similarity between T_i and its remainder non-self subsequences. The threshold δ is computed adaptively and represents the average similarity between normal subsequences, which will be discussed in Sect. 3.3 in details. The anomaly detection algorithm is summarized in Table 1.

Table 1. Anomaly detection algorithm.

Input: a time series T, subsequence length m, δ	
Output: anomaly	
1	anomaly = Ø
2	T = select_candidate (all subsequences)
3	for T_i in T:
4	nonselfList = non-self_subsequences (T_i)
5	flag = False
6	for T_j in nonselfList:
7	sim = similarity(T_i, T_j)
8	if(sim>δ):
9	flag = True break
10	end if
11	end for
12	if (flag == False):
13	anomaly[i] = T_i
14	end if
15	end for
16	return anomaly

3.2   Candidate Anomalies

In order to quickly find out which subsequences are approximately similar and which are different from others, each subsequence is represented by a string. If subsequences are of the same string, they are approximately similar and vice versa.

Firstly we use Piecewise Aggregation Approximation (PAA) to represent each subsequence. In PAA, data is split by fixed windows and the mean of each window makes up a new series. The window size s is a parameter which reflects the degree of data compression. For a subsequence T_i with length m, $T_i = [t_i, t_{i+1}, \ldots t_j, \ldots t_{m+i-1}]$, T_i' is the new subsequence after PAA transformation. $T_i' = [t_p]$, where

$$t_p = \frac{\sum\limits_{j=p}^{p+s-1} t_j}{s} \qquad p = \{i, s+i, 2s+i, \ldots, ks+i\} \quad k = \lfloor m/s \rfloor \qquad (1)$$

The length of T_i' is $\lfloor m/s \rfloor$. In this paper, we set $s = max(4, 0.02 \times m)$.

Secondly, each transformed subsequence T_i' is discretized according to Eq. 2, where the maximum and minimum values in original time series are denoted as *max* and *min* respectively.

$$t_p' = \left\lfloor \frac{t_p - min}{(max - min)/\Delta} \right\rfloor \qquad (2)$$

Keogh figured out that the best value of SAX alphabet size is 3 which could fit any dataset. Thus, we fix $\Delta = 3$. At this step, each subsequence is transformed into a string. The length of string is $\lfloor m/s \rfloor$ and the value of each symbol is $\{0, 1, 2\}$.

Subsequences of same string are similar and vice versa. This idea could be employed to select candidate anomaly subsequences. However, a little difference between two strings, i.e. one or two symbols difference, will not indicate their corresponding subsequences are not similar especially when string is long. Therefore, in our method, subsequences of similar strings are grouped together.

For a string, there are three cases. Firstly, if a string corresponds to only one subsequence, it indicates that this subsequence is quite different from others and is very likely to be anomaly. So it is considered as an anomaly candidate. Secondly, if a string corresponds to multiple non-overlapping subsequences, then these subsequences are similar and they are considered to be normal behavior. Thirdly, if a string corresponds to multiple overlapping subsequences, then concatenate them. And the corresponding long subsequence is regarded as a candidate. For example, if subsequence length is 10, subsequence T_5, T_8, T_{10} are overlapping and they constitute a long subsequence which starts from time step 5 and ends at step 19. Thus the anomaly candidates may of different length in our method.

3.3 Similarity Threshold

Intuitively, an anomaly is not similar with the other subsequences. While for a normal subsequence, there are some subsequences similar with it. These similar subsequences which occur frequently can be regarded as a normal pattern. In a whole time series, there might be multiple normal patterns. The similarity between an anomaly and its non-self subsequences must be lower than the similarity between a normal behavior. In our method, we employ the average of normal behaviors similarity as a threshold, which is defined in Eq. 3.

$$\delta = \frac{\sum\limits_{i=i}^{s} sim(p_i)}{s} \qquad (3)$$

Where p_i represents a normal pattern, s is the number of normal patterns in a whole time series.

Since subsequences of same string are similar, we random select one of them to represent this kind of normal behavior. And the similarity of one normal pattern is computed as follows.

$$sim(p) = \max_{j}(f(T_i, T_j)) \qquad (4)$$

Where f is a similarity function, T_i is a representative subsequence of the normal pattern p and T_j is the non-self subsequence of T_i in whole time series. Here we use the maximum similarity between T_i and its all non-self subsequences.

In this paper, we employ Pearson coefficient as similarity measure rather than the mostly used Euclidian distance or Dynamic time warping (DTW). The latter is computationally expensive. The reason why we don't use Euclidian distance is as follows. Firstly, it is length sensitive. Distance between a long time series is likely to be larger than the distance between short time series. In our method, the anomaly candidates may be of different length due to the concatenation of overlapping subsequences. And it is unfair to compare them by Euclidean distance. Secondly, Euclidean distance is amplitude and offset sensitive which focuses on point-to-point difference. If two subsequences are similar in shape but different in amplitude, i.e. have value offset, their Euclidean distance might be great and this will cause false positive.

4   Experiments and Results

Firstly, we investigate the performance of our method in terms of anomaly detection rate and compare it with a state-of-the-art method SST exemplars based method on the benchmark datasets [3] from diverse domains, including space shuttle, ECG, video surveillance, power demand facility. Secondly, we test the robustness of our method to the parameter subsequence length.

4.1   Results on Public Datasets

For power data, there are three anomalies and our method can detect all of them, which is marked with red line in Fig. 1(a). To test SST exemplars based method, we take subsequence from time step 15000 to 25000 as a training series which does not contain any anomaly and the whole series as a test series. Anomaly detection results are shown in Fig. 1(b) where the top is test series and the bottom is anomaly score given by SST exemplars based method. We can see that the first anomaly (from left to right in Fig. 1 (a)) is not detected by SST exemplars method. What's more, the anomaly score around time step 20000 is close to the third anomaly's score, which is located around time step

35000. That means if the anomaly score threshold (annotated with blue line) is equal to 500, then only the second anomaly is found. If the anomaly score threshold is set 300, the middle part (around time step 20000) will be also determined as anomaly. Thus for SST exemplars based method, the quality of detection results heavily depends on the anomaly score threshold.

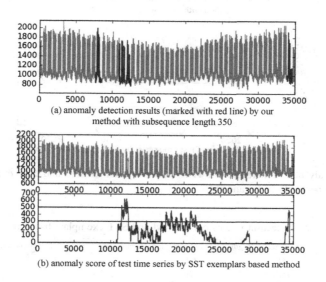

(a) anomaly detection results (marked with red line) by our method with subsequence length 350

(b) anomaly score of test time series by SST exemplars based method

Fig. 1. Anomaly detection results on power dataset by our method and SST exemplars based method are respectively in (a) and (b). (Color figure online)

For Space Shuttle Marotta dataset TEK, we test our method on test time series in [2]. There are three anomalies in total and ground truth is shown with red circle and line in Fig. 2(a). Our method detects the latter two anomalies marked with red line. We found these three anomalies as candidates and the maximum similarity between each of them and their non-self subsequences are respectively 0.964, 0.881, 0.841. And δ is computed to be 0.90, so the first anomaly is missed in our method. The anomaly detection results of SST exemplars based method is shown in Fig. 2(b). We can see that if score threshold is set lower than 100, SST exemplars method detects all these three anomalies. While if score threshold is larger than 300, it will miss the first anomaly.

From experiment results on dataset power and TEK, it can be concluded that for SST exemplars based method, anomaly score threshold has great influence on detection results. However, it is not clear how to get the value of this important parameter. While in our method, the similarity threshold is automatically calculated without domain knowledge.

The detection rate of our method and SST exemplars based method on 24 datasets is shown in Table 2. The results demonstrate that these two methods are of the same anomaly detection rate. However, our method is unsupervised and parameter light comparing with SST exemplars, which makes our method friendly to use.

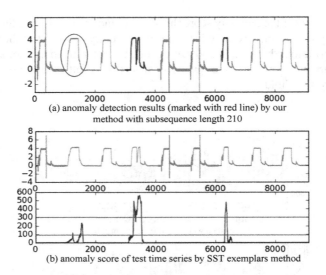

(a) anomaly detection results (marked with red line) by our
method with subsequence length 210

(b) anomaly score of test time series by SST exemplars method

Fig. 2. Anomaly detection results on TEK dataset by our method and SST exemplars based method are respectively in (a) and (b).

Table 2. Detection rate of our method and SST exemplars based method.

Dataset	Time series length	Our method detection rate	SST exemplars detection rate
chfdbchf01_1	3751	1/1	1/1
chfdbchf01_2	3751	1/1	1/1
chfdbchf13_1	3750	1/1	1/1
chfdbchf13_2	3750	1/1	1/1
chfdbchf15_1	15000	1/1	1/1
chfdbchf15_2	15000	1/1	1/1
ltstdb20221_1	3750	1/1	1/1
ltstdb20221_2	3750	1/1	1/1
ltstdb20321_1	3750	1/1	1/1
ltstdb20321_2	3750	1/1	1/1
mitdb100_1	5401	1/1	1/1
mitdb100_2	5401	1/1	1/1
xmitdbx108_1	5400	1/1	1/1
xmitdbx108_2	5400	1/1	1/1
qtdbsel0606_1	3000	1/1	1/1
qtdbsel0606_2	3000	1/1	1/1
qtdbsel102_2	45000	1/1	1/1
nprs44	24125	1/1	1/1
stdb308_1	5400	1/1	1/1
stdb308_2	5400	1/1	1/1
anngun_1	11251	1/1	1/1
anngun_2	11251	1/1	1/1
TEK	9099	2/3	3/3
power data	35040	3/3	2/3
Total		28/29	28/29

4.2   Sensitivity of Parameter Subsequence Length

We investigate the robustness of our method to the variations of subsequence length. Figure 3 presents the anomaly detection results (marked with red line) on some datasets and the corresponding range of subsequences length. For time series chfdbchf13_2, from congestive heart failure database, there is an apparent amplitude anomaly and our method detects the anomaly with subsequence length ranging from 30 to 130. For time series mitdb100_1, it is periodic and the anomaly is the shorter period data. The anomaly detection results coincide with ground truth with subsequence length from 210 to 300. For time series mitdb/x_mitdb/x_108, there are multiple different anomalies. Our method could detect all of them with subsequence length ranging from 150 to 400.

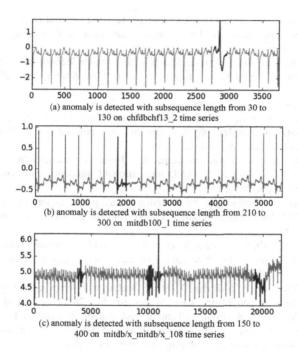

(a) anomaly is detected with subsequence length from 30 to
130 on chfdbchf13_2 time series

(b) anomaly is detected with subsequence length from 210 to
300 on mitdb100_1 time series

(c) anomaly is detected with subsequence length from 150 to
400 on mitdb/x_mitdb/x_108 time series

Fig. 3. Anomaly detection results (marked with red line) and the corresponding range of subsequences length on three datasets. (Color figure online)

5   Conclusion

In this paper, we propose an unsupervised and parameter-lite anomaly detection method. The basic idea is that if the similarity between a subsequence and its nearest neighbor is smaller than the threshold, this subsequence is anomaly. To reduce the pairwise similarity computation, we firstly select candidate anomalies and only need to calculate the similarity between candidates and their corresponding non-self subsequences. Discretized string is employed to identify the normal behaviors and candidate anomalies. What's more, we present how to calculate the similarity threshold in an unsupervised manner. Finally, we conduct experiments on many diverse datasets. From experiment results, we can get the following conclusions. First, comparing with state-of-the-art method, our method reach the same detection rate without any human knowledge. Second, our method is not sensitive to the variations of subsequence length, which is the only one parameter. Thirdly, SST exemplars based method is superior to our method in term of time efficiency. In future work, we will try to improve the speed of the algorithm.

References

1. Keogh, E., Lin, J., Fu, A.: HOT SAX: finding the most unusual time series subsequence: algorithms and applications. In: Proceedings of International Conference on Data Mining, pp. 226–233 (2005)
2. Jones, M., Nikovski, D., Imamura, M., et al.: Exemplar learning for extremely efficient anomaly detection in real-valued time series. Data Min. Knowl. Disc. **30**(6), 1427–1454 (2016)
3. http://www.cs.ucr.edu/~eamonn/discords/
4. Liu, B., Chen, H., Sharma, A., et al.: Modeling heterogeneous time series dynamics to profile big sensor data in complex physical systems. In: Proceedings of IEEE International Conference on Big Data, pp. 631–638 (2013)
5. Keogh, E., Lonardi, S., Ratanamahatana, C.: Towards parameter-free data mining. In: Proceedings of the 10th ACM SIGKDD International Conference on Knowledge Discovery and Data Mining, pp. 206–215 (2004)
6. Ma, J., Perkins, S.: Online novelty detection on temporal sequences. In: Proceedings of ACM SIGKDD International Conference on Knowledge Discovery and Data Mining, pp. 613–618 (2003)
7. Pankaj, M., Lovekesh, V., Gautam, S., et al.: Long short term memory networks for anomaly detection in time series. In: Proceedings of European Symposium on Artificial Neural Networks, pp. 89–94 (2015)
8. Appice, A., Guccione, P., Malerba, D., et al.: Dealing with temporal and spatial correlations to classify outliers in geophysical data streams. Inf. Sci. **285**(1), 162–180 (2014)
9. Laptev, N., Amizadeh, S., Flint, I.: Generic and scalable framework for automated time-series anomaly detection. In: Proceedings of ACM SIGKDD International Conference on Knowledge Discovery and Data Mining, pp. 1939–1947 (2015)
10. Zheng, D., Li, F., Zhao, T.: Self-adaptive statistical process control for anomaly detection in time series. Expert. Syst. Appl. **57**(1), 324–336 (2016)
11. Wang, H., Tang, M., Park, Y., et al.: Locality statistics for anomaly detection in time series of graphs. IEEE Trans. Signal Process. **62**(3), 703–717 (2014)
12. Ma, J., Sun, L., Wang, H., et al.: Supervised anomaly detection in uncertain pseudoperiodic data streams. ACM Trans. Internet Technol. **16**(1), 4–24 (2016)
13. Burbeck, K., Nadjm-Tehrani, S.: Adaptive real-time anomaly detection with incremental clustering. Inf. Secur. Techn. Rep. **12**(1), 56–67 (2007)
14. Izakian, H., Pedrycz, W.: Anomaly detection and characterization in spatial time series data: a cluster-centric approach. IEEE Trans. Fuzzy Syst. **22**(6), 1612–1624 (2014)
15. Hsiao, K., Xu, K., Calder, J., et al.: Multicriteria similarity-based anomaly detection using pareto depth analysis. IEEE Trans. Neural Netw. Learn. Syst. **27**(6), 1307–1321 (2016)

Big Science Data Framework

Performance Prediction in Nuclear Materials by Using a Collaborative Framework of Supercomputing, Big Data and Artificial Intelligence

Danning Li[1,2](✉) ⓘ, Dandan Chen[1,2] ⓘ, and Changjun Hu[1,2]

[1] School of Computer and Communication Engineering,
University of Science and Technology Beijing, Beijing 100083, China
lemon20171020@gmail.com
[2] Beijing Key Laboratory of Knowledge Engineering for Material Science,
Beijing, China

Abstract. Irradiation effects of materials have a direct influence on the safety of nuclear reactors. Multiscale simulations are often used to understand the evolution of material irradiation damage. With the improvement of memory and computational power, the multiscale simulation puts forward high demands for supercomputing, big data, and artificial intelligence. This paper explores a collaborative framework of supercomputing, big data, and artificial intelligence to perform multiscale simulations for irradiation damage and to predict the macroscopic properties of materials. First, this paper proposes a general collaborative framework about model-calculation-analysis, based on the collaboration of SC, BD, and AI. Next, for multiscale simulation of materials, we design a specific collaborative framework inheriting the above general one. Furthermore, this paper presents a framework instance of microscopic simulations for material swelling under neutron irradiation. Finally, this paper gives two case studies. The first case study is a nuclear material simulation program by using the collaboration of supercomputing and big data. The second case study is a prediction for irradiation hardening by using the collaboration of big data and artificial intelligence. The proposed framework not only provides insights into the performance prediction of nuclear materials, but also can be applied to other application domains.

Keywords: Collaborative framework · Supercomputing · Big data
Artificial intelligence · Performance prediction of nuclear materials

1 Introduction

1.1 A Subsection Sample

Stable properties of nuclear materials (e.g., reactor pressure vessels, fuel claddings) under irradiation are the basis for ensuring the safety of nuclear

Supported by University of Science and Technology Beijing (USTB).

© Springer Nature Singapore Pte Ltd. 2019
R. Ren et al. (Eds.): SDBA 2018, CCIS 911, pp. 97–110, 2019.
https://doi.org/10.1007/978-981-13-5910-1_9

reactors. Since the dawn of supercomputing (SC), computational and memory power are rapidly increasing. The development of material simulations has entered into a new stage with lots of breakthroughs [1–3]. Massive data has been accumulated by long-term simulating and experimenting in nuclear materials over time. It's going from the traditional research phase to a new phase where big data (BD) drives new material discovery [4]. In recent years, with the popularity of artificial intelligence (AI), a increasingly obvious trend is that intelligent methods are introduced into the study of material prediction [5]. Supercomputing, big data and artificial intelligence have all achieved great results in the field of nuclear materials. However, as the research moves along, material simulations raise new demands and challenges for SC, BD, and AI.

As far as the current supercomputers [6] are concerned, whether the storage or computing power cannot meet the needs of simulations. For example, the refined simulation of molecular dynamics (MD) requires 10^{20} atoms in spatial scale [7]. Besides, the simulation of irradiation swelling in reactors usually have a direct requirement for simulating the evolution of trillions of atoms in microseconds [8]. Nowadays, given the simulation demand for supercomputing have increased from 1PFlops to 1EFlops in nuclear materials [9]. As a result, it's urgent to develop exascale supercomputers [10]. In addition, material scientists in different fields hold different views on the same material, which makes material data complex and diverse. In order to address this problem, a unified domain data model should be established to efficiently store multiple types of material data. Furthermore, artificial intelligence based on material data has been more widely used for material research. For example, a technique called artificial neural network (ANN) [11] is able to build a model to predict the change of the Charpy ductile-brittle transition temperature (ΔDBTT) for irradiated low-activation martensitic steels [12]. Another example is that pattern recognition technology has applied to segment material metallographic images [13]. Previous artificial intelligence is limited by the computing power at that time. But now, it has become a trend to develop advanced AI due to supercomputing.

The organization of the paper is as follows. Section 2 presents some related work about classical collaborations. In Sect. 3, we propose a general collaborative framework of SC, BD and AI, and materialize the framework to satisfy the needs of multiscale simulation in nuclear materials. For one specific case of swelling for nuclear materials, a possible application is discussed by using the framework. In next section, based on the previous related work and collaborative framework, we conduct two case studies that are described detailedly in Sect. 4.1 and in Sect. 4.2. In the end, Sect. 5 makes a conclusion and discusses the future research.

2   Related Work

2.1   Collaboration of SC and BD

A supercomputer is usually a tool for processing big data. Supercomputers are able to handle big data quickly and parallel. Besides they can store massive data and meet the communication needs for frequent exchange between data.

Conversely, big data technologies can be used as the guiding tools for supercomputing. For example, a MapReduce technology is used to optimize parallel storage strategies [14]. Another technology named incremental processing provides a valid solution for the dynamic update of memory data [15]. The simulation results in massive data by supercomputing, which requires big data management. Taking the coupled of MD and Kinetic Monte Carlo (KMC) [16] simulation as an example, each particle requires 100 bytes of computer memory [17]. MD needs to simulate about 10^{20} particles [7] and KMC needs to simulate about 10^{17} particles, for which required computer memory is more than 10^{10} TB. In principle, most of simulation programs store the data in master-slave memory by defining arrays, resulting in many of the problems such as insufficient memory, communication overheads. It's necessary to introduce the technology of big data management into solving above problems. Therefore, material simulations require big data management, and big data processing needs resources of supercomputing.

2.2   Collaboration of BD and AI

For one thing, big data is the basis of developing artificial intelligence. Data mining and logical judgement based on big data technologies, such as distributed storage and load balance, combined with interactive technology to form artificial intelligence. For example, massive data is the guarantee of effective training for deep learning. For another thing, artificial intelligence technologies provide new insights for big data processing, including classification, clustering, regression, optimization algorithm and so on. After acquiring massive data, artificial intelligence can analyze and summarize some characteristics from them, and then make reactions and predictions. In materials, Raccuglia et al. [18] used machine learning algorithm to predict the synthesis of new materials from failed experimental data, and the accuracy of machine learning model on prediction exceeded in that of experienced chemists in experiments. Consequently, big data and artificial intelligence cannot be separated from each other.

2.3   Collaboration of SC and AI

On the one hand, supercomputing can implement AI as a tool, for example, large-scale deep learning calls for the support of computational power on supercomputers. Watson [19], a supercomputer built by IBM, implements a powerful natural language processing algorithm. It is able to communicate with people freely. On the other hand, some smart optimization algorithms can improve the computing power of supercomputers. For example, the LDA algorithm [20] can effectively solve the problem of memory limitations on the GPU. The packing algorithm for maximum coverage proposed by Jung et al. [21] can effectively address the allocation problem among computational nodes of supercomputer, whose performance has improved by 60% compared with other algorithms. The development of artificial intelligence and supercomputing complement each other.

3   Methodology

3.1   A General Collaborative Framework of SC, BD, and AI

As discussed previously, supercomputing is able to deal with big data in parallel, whereas the massive data produced by large-scale scientific simulation requires database management technology, and artificial intelligence needs massive data as a support. For the purpose of solving the problems of computation, data, and model optimizating, a scientific and general framework is proposed about model-calculation-analysis, based on the collaboration of supercomputings, big data technologies, and artificial intelligence methods. That is models-calculation, calculations-data, data-analysis, analysis results optimizing the model as detailed in Fig. 1.

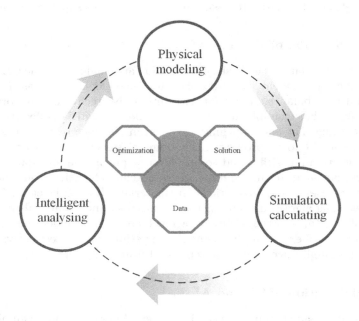

Fig. 1. A general collaborative framework of SC, BD and AI

For example, the multiscale simulation of nuclear materials covers different models and calculation approaches from atomic scale to mesoscopic scale, and then to macro scale. In regard to our new method, we use MD, KMC, RT, FEM and other computer simulation technologies to solve some physical models. Besides a large amount of data is generated during the computational simulation. In order to manage massive data, Hu et al. [22] proposed a new concept of virtual data space. It's a virtual data space model for large-scale data access of material science, and it's also a combination of data space and complex data management. A virtual data control model needs to be built from cache, then from slave memory, main memory, local storage, and finally to cluster storage in it. Consequently big data technology is required and used to achieve efficient memory access. At the same time, the simulation data is statistically analyzed by intelligent methods such as neural network and deep learning. At the end, the knowledge hidden by statistical analysis is able to further revise and optimize the multiscale computing model to improve the accuracy of simulation. What counts is the framework applied not only in nuclear materials but also in other fields.

3.2   A Collaborative Framework of SC, BD, and AI in Nuclear Materials

Irradiation experiments of nuclear materials are usually difficult, costly and time-consuming. In order to study the microscopic evolution of materials, predict macroscopic mechanical properties, and meet the simulation demand of high precision, multiscale simulation modeling approach [23] is usually used, such as RPV-1 and RPV-2 [24,25], from European projects. RPV-1 achieved multiscale simulation of irradiation hardening on RPV steel. Combining with the research background, the effect of irradiation on material properties spans large temporal and spatial scales [8]. It not only brings forward the demand for high precision and large-scale simulation, but also needs to carry out multiscale simulation for exascale computing with the help of Sunway TaihuLight [26] and Milkyway-2 [27] supercomputer. Therefore, this paper designs a specific collaborative framework of SC, BD, and AI, which is used for multiscale simulation of irradiation damage in nuclear materials (see Fig. 2).

Figure 2 displays a new framework, where the multiscale simulation contains MD method, KMC method, rate theory (RT) method [28] and finite element method (FEM) [29], etc. MD can simulate the process of cascade collision. KMC is used to simulate the defect annealing process. The long process of defects evolution is simulated by RT and FEM. For the large amounts of data generated by simulating such as defect size and concentration, the distributed storage and virtual data space relying on supercomputers are used. High-performance network is used to achieve efficient data fetching. Big data technology is applied to manage collected data (e.g. data from irradiation experiment, material composition, machining technology) and to simulate data. Furthermore, a domain data model should be established, and form a material database. At this point, we conduct large-scale molecular dynamics simulation with the collaboration of SC and BD, and we use the collaboration of BD and AI to implement the prediction of irradiation hardening. Correlative studies will be described detailedly in Sect. 4.

In principle, with regard to the specific collaborative framework, all three complement to each other for the multiscale simulation research in irradiation damage of materials, and the collaboration of SC, BD, and AI provides a more efficient and precise solution to predict material properties.

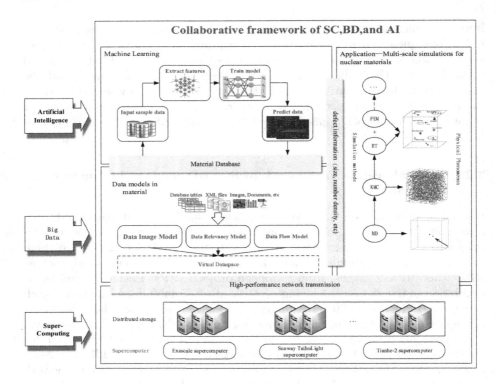

Fig. 2. A specific collaborative framework inheriting the general one for multiscale simulation of materials

3.3   Performance Prediction in Nuclear Materials by the Framework

The new framework proposed above can be applied to the prediction of irradiation swelling. It can be observed in Fig. 3. Nuclear materials produce two types of point defects due to neutron irradiation, which are interstitial and vacancy-type defects. Most of point defects will be combined, but uncombined point defects will diffuse and cluster. Because dislocation and grain boundary are stronger than vacancies at the ability of absorbing interstitials, the vacancy defects accumulate or form complexes with gas atoms such as He, and constantly gather and grow up to form voids. Eventually these will cause irradiation swelling of materials. The swelling of materials is determined by the volume fraction of voids, given by the following formula:

$$\frac{\Delta V}{V} = \int_{R=1nm}^{R=\infty} \frac{4}{3}\pi R_{void}^3 N_{void} dR, \tag{1}$$

where R_{void} is the size of void (i.e., vacancy cluster), N_{void} is the number density of void.

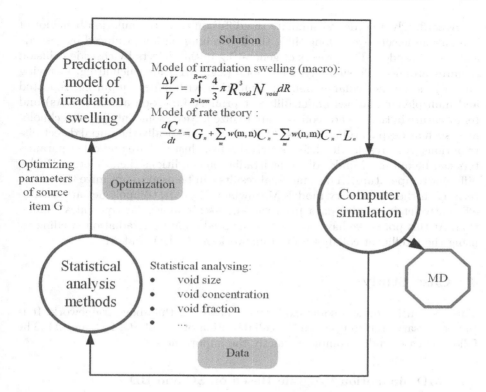

Fig. 3. Prediction model of irradiation swelling based on the collaboration framework of SC, BD, and AI

It can be seen, the size and number density of voids are critical determinants of swelling, and these parameters need to be calculated by the mesoscale simulation methods (e.g., RT, KMC). Illustrated by a case of RT, the model is used to describe the evolution of cluster size concentration:

$$\frac{dC_n}{dt} = G_n + \sum_k w(k, n)C_k - \sum_k w(n, k)C_n - L_n, \tag{2}$$

where C_n is the concentration of a vacancy cluster of size n. The first term on the right side of Eq. (2), G_n, is the generation rate of a cluster. The second and third term correspond to reactions of conversion to and from a cluster of size n, respectively. The fourth term represents the absorption term of inherent defects (e.g., grain boundary, dislocation, dislocation loop, bubble) in materials. G_n in Eq. (2) can be expressed as,

$$G_1 = G_{NRT}(1 - \varepsilon_r)(1 - \varepsilon_{VCL}), \tag{3}$$

where G_{NRT} is the damage rate, $(1 - \varepsilon_r)$ is the cascade efficiency, ε_{VCL} is the shares of the vacancies during cascade collisions.

Accordingly, in order to simulate the diffusion and accumulation behavior of irradiation defects over a long time, the defect information produced by cascade collision is needed. The process of generating initial defects by cascade collision requires atomic-scale simulation methods (e.g., MD) for calculating. Carrying out large-scale molecular dynamics simulation with supercomputing, repeated and multiple simulations under different primary knock-on atoms (PKAs) and temperature in the cascade collision are realized. Next, some intelligent technologies, such as deep learning, are used to analyze statistically the initial defect distributions. As a result, the defect survival rates, cluster share and other parameters can be obtained under different irradiation conditions (i.e., different PKAs, different temperature). The analytical results can be used to optimize the source term G in the rate theory model. Meanwhile, big data technologies are used to efficiently fetch massive data from the large-scale molecular dynamics simulation. At this point, we have conducted the prediction for irradiation swelling by using the intelligent collaboration framework of SC, BD, and AI.

4   Case Study

This section introduces some exploration based on the above framework. It is the neccessary step to practice the collaboration of two of SC, BD, and AI. The following case studies complete exactly the important step.

4.1   MD Simulation Program Based on SC and BD

Atomic-level simulation plays an important role in understanding irradiation effects of materials. Molecular dynamics, as an effective atomic-level simulation method, has become as important as experiments in material science. Large-scale MD simulation is carried out relying on SC and BD, which is conducive to deeply understand micro-level-material. We propose a new data structure for accessing massive simulation data, which named lattice neighbor list [30]. Based on the new data structure, we have developed a new MD software named Crystal MD [17], and it shows a good simulation effect.

For performing a bigger scale of MD simulation, we focused on the microevolutionary characteristics of BCC metal under irradiation environment: atoms were constrained near every lattice point, and barely moved throughout the MD simulation. In Crystal MD, according to the spatial distribution of atoms, our lattice neighbor list stored the atomic information (e.g., position, velocity) in the corresponding arrays in order. Meanwhile, when atoms moved away the lattice points, the program would allocate additional memory to store them. For developing large-scale parrallel MD simulation program with Crystal MD, we used the standard domain decomposition to divide the simulation box. The atoms to be sent to neighbor processor as their ghost area were fixed. The information of above atoms were exchanged between processes by communication.

The experiments of Crystal MD were proformed on Tianhe-2 supercomputer, which focused on memory usage and scalability. For testing the memory usage of Crystal MD, we compared with LAMMPS [31] and IMD [32] with case of same core and atom number. They fully filled the memory that each CPU core could reach to. It can be seen from Table 1 our method took much less memory on multi-core clusters.

Table 1. Memory usage on Tianhe-2 MD simulation software.

Name	CPU cores	Calculation scale (BCC length)	Memory usage
Crystal MD	100	250000000 (500)	0.5664 (G/core)
LAMMPS	100	250000000 (500)	1.2 (G/core)
IMD	100	250000000 (500)	0.7656 (G/core)

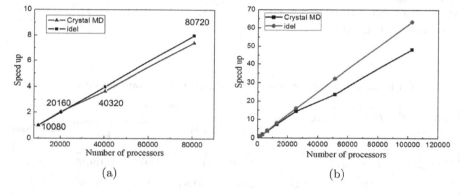

Fig. 4. Scalability of Crystal MD on Tianhe-2 (a) and Sunway TaihuLight (b).

For testing the scalability of Crystal MD, we tested it on Tianhe-2 and Sunway TaihuLight supercomputer. We used the scenario of Fe at the temperature of 600 K, and ran 10 steps. The simulated box was $10000 \times 10000 \times 1000$ (in the unit of BCC length) with 2×10^{11} atoms. The amount of cores were from 10 080 to 80 640 on Tianhe-2 supercomputer, and the amount of cores were from 1600 to 102400 on Sunway TaihuLight supercomputer. In order to test the largest scale that could be simulated by Crystal MD, 102400 CPU cores (on Sunway Taihu-Light supercomputer) were used in the experiment. In addition, the memory of each node was filled. The consequence of simulation indicates that the largest scale is 4×10^{12} atoms, which extends the reach of MD simulation (10^{12} atoms). It can be concluded from Fig. 4 that our Crystal MD has a great scalability in massively parallel case.

4.2 Prediction of Irradiation Hardening Based on BD and AI

The reactor pressure vessel (RPV) is exclusive component that cannot be replaced during a reactor lifetime. One of the main irradiation effects is irradiation hardening for RPV. It results from that the defect clusters produced

by irradiation block the movement of dislocation, consequently forming hardening, which indicates that the yield stress of materials increases rapidly. Artificial
intelligence technologies that rely on big data, such as machine learning, have
become an effective means for prediction of material properties. Relying on the
collaboration of BD and AI, we have achieved the prediction and analysis of
irradiation hardening for low-activation ferritic/martensitic steel (RAFM).

Table 2. Example datasets of materials.

Data set	Count record	Train record	Test record	Count attribute
MAP_DATA_THERMAL	391	293	98	15
MAP_DATA_ADI_RETAINED	1910	1432	478	10
MAP_STEEL_IRR_AUSTENTIC	359	269	90	13
MAP_STEEL_IRR_CHARPY	455	341	114	17
MAP_STEEL_IRR_RAFM	1811	1358	453	36

Table 3. Test errors of typical ML algorithms in example datasets

MSE / $10^3 MPa$ Algorithm Data Set	MLP	SVM	Decision Tree	Random Forest	AdaBoost
MAP_DATA_THERMAL	0.1476	0.1222	0.0934	**0.0835**	0.0871
MAP_DATA_ADI_RETAINED	0.2944	**0.0131**	0.0165	0.0140	0.0423
MAP_STEEL_IRR_AUSTENTIC	0.4660	0.2506	0.1303	**0.0633**	0.0786
MAP_STEEL_IRR_CHARPY	0.1043	0.0101	0.0064	**0.0054**	0.0404
MAP_STEEL_IRR_RAFM	0.1490	0.1896	0.1259	**0.1137**	0.1251

There are many machine learning algorithms about prediction of material
property, but single algorithm cannot obtain the best predictive effect for all of
materials. Therefore, we used more than one algorithm to predict the change
of the yield stress for RAFM under irradiation, such as multilayer perceptron (MLP), support vector machine (SVM), decision tree, random forest and
adaboost, and then compared their prediction accuracy. For this research, the
data about material properties from MAP Program & Data Library Contents of
University of Cambridge [33] was analyzed, which was also used in [34] the work
of Kemp et al. [35]. The relevant dataset is shown in Table 2. In each experiment, the training set and test set are randomly selected. The final result is
the average of 100 experimental results, and the optimal result is highlighted
in bold (see Table 3). The result of Table 3 demonstrates that the tree model
(the latter three algorithms) generally achieves better effect. Accordingly, the
tree model was chosen to explore the change of tensile properties of RAFM. We

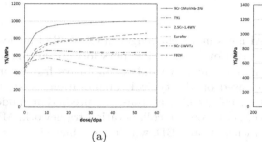
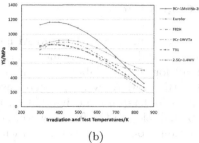

(a)   (b)

Fig. 5. Tree model prediction for the yield stress of different RAFM steels, as a function of irradiation dose with $T_{test} = T_{irr} = 400K$ (a), or a function of temperature with does was 2 dpa (b).

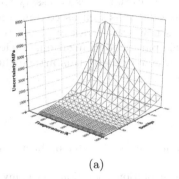
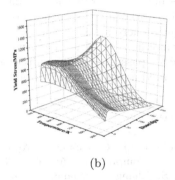

(a)   (b)

Fig. 6. Tree model prediction and uncertainty for the yield stress of Eurofer'97, as a function of irradiation dose and temperature.

established a mapping relationship between the irradiation dose or temperature and the yield stress for RAFM steels, which include Eurofer'97, F82H, T91, 9Cr-1MovVNb-2Ni, 9Cr-1WVTa and 2.5Cr-1.4WV. The prediction results are consistent with the study of Kemp et al. [34].

Figure 5(a) shows that the yield stress increase rapidly under low dose irradiation. But after reaching a certain degree, it is not evident that the change of yield stress brought about by increasing irradiation dose. It's seen from Fig. 5(b) that the higher the temperature is, the lower the yield stress is. Besides irradiation will cause rapid hardening of steels even if low doses. After that, Eurofer'97 was selected to analyze yield stress under different irradiation dose and temperature. Figure 6 shows that the predictions and corresponding uncertainties are estimated at T_{test}, T_{irr} (300–900K) and dose (0–200dpa) . Uncertainties of area outside the training set have that are comparable to or larger than yield stress. Therefore, these uncertainties represent regions where experiments might successfully be carried out, and indicates that predictions in these regions should be considered carefully until corroborated.

5   Conclusion

The application of SC, BD, and AI faces many challenges in the field of nuclear materials, and the performance prediction of materials puts forward an urgent demand for their collaboration. In this paper, a valid collaborative framework of SC, BD, and AI was designed based on the typical collaboration. Next, in order to understand the irradiation effects of materials, an prediction model will be modeled in the future work. Based on the collaboration framework, MD simulation program was developed with SC and BD, which has achieved 4×10^{12} atoms of simulation scale on the Sunway TaihuLight supercomputer. We also have predicted irradiation hardening of RAFM steels with BD and AI.

The new collaboration framework opens a new door to the material science, which goes from microscopic to macroscopic evolution. To deeply understand the mechanism of irradiation damage in nuclear materials, it is necessary to pay attention to both physical models and massive data, as well as computational efficiency. There are also challenges about this new framework applying to the research of irradiation damage, such as exascale parallel optimization, efficiently parameter passing among multiscale coupling. Accordingly, this article should be regarded as an early step in long-term efforts.

References

1. Wang, J., Liu, C., Huang, Y.: Auto tuning for new energy dispatch problem. Future Gener. Comput. Syst. **54**, 501–506 (2016)
2. Li, S., Zhang, Y., Xiang, C., Shi, L.: Fast convolution operations on many-core architectures, pp. 316–323 (2015)
3. Shigang, L., Torsten, H., Chunjin, H., Marc, S.: Cluster Computing, pp. 1–17 (2014)
4. Agrawal, A., Choudhary, A.: Perspective: materials informatics and big data: realization of the "fourth paradigm" of science in materials science, vol. 4, p. 053208 (2016)
5. Ramprasad, R., Batra, R., Pilania, G., Mannodikanakkithodi, A., Kim, C.: Machine learning in materials informatics: recent applications and prospects. Mater. Mater. Sci. **3**(1), Article number 54 (2017)
6. Feldman, M.: China tops supercomputer rankings with new 93-petaflop machine (2017)
7. Rosner, R., et al.: Science based nuclear energy systems enabled by advanced modeling and simulation at the extreme scale. In: ASCR Scientific Grand Challenges Workshop Series. Technical report (2009)
8. Bacon, D.J., Osetsky, Y.N.: Multiscale modelling of radiation damage in metals: from defect generation to material properties. Mater. Sci. Eng. A **365**(1–2), 46–56 (2004)
9. Kothe, D.B.: CASL: the consortium for advanced simulation of light water reactors. Bull. Am. Phys. Soc. **55** (2010)
10. Bergman, K., et al.: Exascale computing study: technology challenges in achieving exascale systems. Defense Advanced Research Projects Agency Information Processing Techniques Office (DARPA IPTO). Technical report, vol. 15 (2008)

11. Hertz, J.A.: Introduction to the Theory of Neural Computation. CRC Press, Boca Raton (2018)
12. Cottrell, G., Kemp, R., Bhadeshia, H., Odette, G., Yamamoto, T.: Neural network analysis of charpy transition temperature of irradiated low-activation martensitic steels. J. Nucl. Mater. **367**, 603–609 (2007)
13. de Albuquerque, V.H.C., de Alexandria, A.R., Cortez, P.C., Tavares, J.M.R.: Evaluation of multilayer perceptron and self-organizing map neural network topologies applied on microstructure segmentation from metallographic images. NDT & E Int. **42**(7), 644–651 (2009)
14. Ji, C., Li, Y., Qiu, W., Awada, U., Li, K.: Big data processing in cloud computing environments. In: 12th International Symposium on Pervasive Systems, Algorithms and Networks (ISPAN), PP. 17–23. IEEE (2012)
15. Bhatotia, P., Wieder, A., Rodrigues, R., Acar, U.A., Pasquin, R.: Incoop: MapReduce for incremental computations. In: Proceedings of the 2nd ACM Symposium on Cloud Computing, p. 7. ACM (2011)
16. Voter, A.F.: Introduction to the Kinetic Monte Carlo method. In: Sickafus, K.E., Kotomin, E.A., Uberuaga, B.P. (eds.) Radiation Effects in Solids. NATO Science Series, vol. 235, pp. 1–23. Springer, Dordrecht (2007). https://doi.org/10.1007/978-1-4020-5295-8_1
17. Hu, C., et al.: Crystal MD: the massively parallel molecular dynamics software for metal with BCC structure. Comput. Phys. Commun. **211**, 73–78 (2017)
18. Raccuglia, P., et al.: Machine-learning-assisted materials discovery using failed experiments. Nature **533**(7601), 73 (2016)
19. High, R.: The Era of Cognitive Systems: An Inside Look at IBM Watson and How it Works. IBM Corporation Redbooks, New York (2012)
20. Yan, F., Xu, N., Qi, Y.: Parallel inference for latent Dirichlet allocation on graphics processing units. In: Advances in Neural Information Processing Systems, pp. 2134–2142 (2009)
21. Jung, G., Gnanasambandam, N., Mukherjee, T.: Synchronous parallel processing of big-data analytics services to optimize performance in federated clouds. In: 2012 IEEE 5th International Conference on Cloud Computing (CLOUD), pp. 811–818. IEEE (2012)
22. Hu, C., Li, Y., Cheng, X., Liu, Z.: A virtual dataspaces model for large-scale materials scientific data access. Future Gener. Comput. Syst. **54**, 456–468 (2016)
23. Wirth, B., Odette, G., Marian, J., Ventelon, L., Young-Vandersall, J., Zepeda-Ruiz, L.: Multiscale modeling of radiation damage in FE-based alloys in the fusion environment. J. Nucl. Mater. **329**, 103–111 (2004)
24. Jumel, S., et al.: Simulation of irradiation effects in reactor pressure vessel steels: the reactor for virtual experiments (REVE) project. J. Test. Eval. **30**(1), 37–46 (2002)
25. Jumel, S., Van-Duysen, J.C.: Rpv-1: a virtual test reactor to simulate irradiation effects in light water reactor pressure vessel steels. J. Nucl. Mater. **340**(2–3), 125–148 (2005)
26. Fu, H., et al.: The sunway taihulight supercomputer: system and applications. Sci. China Inf. Sci. **59**(7), 072001 (2016)
27. Liao, X., Xiao, L., Yang, C., Lu, Y.: Milkyway-2 supercomputer: system and application. Front. Comput. Sci. **8**(3), 345–356 (2014)
28. Ghoniem, N.M.: Clustering theory of atomic defects. Radiat. Eff. Defects Solids **148**(1–4), 269–318 (1999)
29. Rao, S.S.: The Finite Element Method in Engineering. Butterworth-Heinemann, Boston (2017)

30. Bai, H., Hu, C., He, X., Zhang, B., Wang, J.: Crystal MD: molecular dynamic simulation software for metal with BCC structure. In: Chen, W., et al. (eds.) BDTA 2015. CCIS, vol. 590, pp. 247–258. Springer, Singapore (2016). https://doi.org/10.1007/978-981-10-0457-5_23

31. Lammps manual. http://lammps.sandia.gov/

32. Stadler, J., Mikulla, R., Trebin, H.-R.: IMD: a software package for molecular dynamics studies on parallel computers. Int. J. Mod. Phys. C 8(05), 1131–1140 (1997)

33. Map program & data library contents. https://www.phase-trans.msm.cam.ac.uk/map/map.html

34. Kemp, R., Cottrell, G., Bhadeshia, H., Odette, G., Yamamoto, T., Kishimoto, H.: Neural-network analysis of irradiation hardening in low-activation steels. J. Nucl. Mater. 348(3), 311–328 (2006)

Multi-domain and Sub-role Oriented Software Architecture for Managing Scientific Big Data

Qi Sun⑩, Yue Liu(✉)⑩, Wenjie Tian⑩, Yike Guo⑩, and Jiawei Lu⑩

School of Computer Engineering and Science, Shanghai University, Shanghai, China
sunqichn@163.com, yliu@staff.shu.edu.cn, tianwenjie1997@163.com,
y.guo@imperial.ac.uk, jiaweifirst@gmail.com

Abstract. The existing Scientific Data Management Systems (SDMSs) usually focus on a single domain and the interaction pattern of each subsystem is complex. What's more, the heterogeneity and multi-source of Scientific Big Data (SBD), resulting in a wide variety of databases, scientific devices and functional areas, make the incompatibility and conflict between system modules inevitable. In this context, the paper focuses on the design and technology requirements of a multi-domain and sub-role oriented software architecture. Through integrating multiple databases, third-party systems and related tools, this architecture realizes both the storage and the sharing of multi-domain and multi-type SBD. Particularly, this architecture is divided into four independent functional areas and corresponding roles are designed, which enhances the decoupling and extensibility of the architecture. In addition, this paper has a formal description of the partition design from the perspective of role. On this basis, this paper also shows the typical application scenarios under different roles. The rationality and comprehensiveness of the proposed architecture are proved by describing the architectures design and technology.

Keywords: Software architecture · Role · REST · Scientific big data

1 Introduction

The development of instruments and computing facilities leads to the geometric increase of scientific data, for example, the Large Synoptic Survey Telescope (LSST) in the field of astronomy generates 15–30 TB raw data every night [9]; the Large Hadron Collider (LHC) in the field of high energy physics generates 40PB of experimental data each year [1]. Similar trends have also been observed in life sciences [3], earth sciences [11], biology [2], and so on. At the same time, due to the complexity of scientific experiments, SBD often presents the characteristics of high dimension and complex structure.

In recent years, many institutions have developed varied SDMS for managing SBD. Sequoia 2000 is a system for studying global change information such as

© Springer Nature Singapore Pte Ltd. 2019
R. Ren et al. (Eds.): SDBA 2018, CCIS 911, pp. 111–122, 2019.
https://doi.org/10.1007/978-981-13-5910-1_10

environmental pollution and global warming [5], its large capacity, fast storage engine and visualization tools meet the practical needs of Geoscience; NASA and IBM have developed Paradise for managing large-scale geographic information data [4,15], focusing on data storage and processing technologies rather than data modeling or query; Gray developed SkyServer, a SDMS for SDSS data, to manage TB scale astronomical images and process data [8]. StoneBraker et al developed a data management and analysis software system, SciDB, which focus on the analysis and processing of SBD [12]. Aiming at the complexity of SBD computation, Apach presents a big data high-performance computing framework, Hama [13], which provides a global synchronous parallel computing model and a graph model for scientific computing. In China, especially during the 12th Five-Year Plan, the application of SBD has also made a lot of achievements, such as the neutrino experimental database and the animal subject database. In addition, there are a series of big data benchmarks for data testing to better understand the nature of scientific big data [6,7,10,16].

These SDMSs have played a great role in the management of SBD, but most of them are oriented to a single field and do not have access to third-party management systems, which means that there is no common management of multi-domain data and cross-domain data sharing. In addition, most of these systems are based on certain types of databases, such as relational databases, which are easy to use and maintain but cannot satisfy the requirement of storage and analysis, while non-relational databases are easy to extend, however, when storing and processing SBD, the natural model structure of the data is often changed, which makes subsequent data management and the development of corresponding analysis software too complicated. Finally, because of the complexity of the SBD, the interaction pattern of each module is very intricate, which results in the poor decoupling and expansibility of system, and the modification of one module may leads to the modification of several corresponding modules. These deficiencies create obstacles to the wider and more efficient use of SBD [14].

Therefore, the paper presents a multi-domain and sub-role oriented architecture, and analyses the architecture framework and technology selection from the technical perspective. In the second section of this paper, the design scheme of architecture will be put forward. Third section will formalize the role division of architecture, and describe the communication between roles in the architecture. The deployment of architecture and the selection of its technical requirements will be presented in section four. The fifth section will show the typical application scenarios of the architecture under different roles. The conclusion and future work will be given in seventh six.

2   Architecture of Scientific Big Data Management System

The architecture is consisted of four independent areas (see Fig. 1): Storage and Access Function Area (SAA), Analysis Function Area (AFA), Query Function

Area (QFA), and Basic Service Function Area (BSFA). The design and function of the four areas are independent of each other, and the decoupling of architecture is achieved by using RESTFul interfaces to integrate these areas.

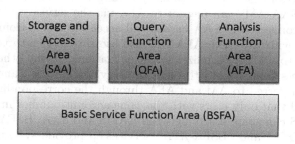

Fig. 1. Four areas of the architecture

Each areas has its own sub-modules and corresponding components. Figure 2 is the software architecture diagram, showing the internal composition of each area and interaction with other areas through interfaces. SAA is responsible for storing various types of SBD to solve the heterogeneous problem. AFA is composed of different scientific experimental tools, which are responsible for carrying out scientific experiments in various fields. The data in SAA and experiments in AFA can be queried and visualized in QFA. BSFA provides related functions to the above areas to maintain the operation of the entire architecture.

SAA is built on various types of databases and distributed file systems to store assets, including relational and non-relational SBD, algorithms such as data mining and domain methods, as well as External Asset Management System (EAMS). In addition, metadata and user information are stored here.

QFA plays a "bridge" role in the whole architecture. In this area, user can query and visualize the assets. It should be noted that QFA is composed of two sub-modules: an Asset Manager (AM) and a Visualizer. AM can be viewed as the "front face" of architecture, it supports a range of asset management operations, such as asset upload and download, quality testing and sharing setting, etc. The Visualizer supports the further display of assets through related devices.

Integration between these two sub-modules is accomplished in the following ways: in order to display asset information, the Visualizer requests the service "AM-Visualizer" through an interface, which is provided by AM, to get the assets and import them into chart generator.

AFA focuses on the scientific experimental analysis of assets by using the integrated methods in the system. The methods here include the special methods in various fields as well as the general machine learning algorithms. Scientists should choose the corresponding methods according to their needs to construct unique scientific experiments.

The fourth area is BSFA. As the base area of the whole architecture, BSFA provides system basic services and resource management functions to the other three areas, and maintains the operation of the architecture.

In the proposed architecture, the interoperability between all four areas is achieved by using RESTFul Interfaces and related services. AM is the requester of SAA service "SAA-AM", which can transfer assets stored in SAA to AM, while AM integrates operations related to asset management. The assets received by using service "SAA-AM" can be sent to AFA via the service "AM-AFA". AFA is not directly connected to SAA because all necessary assets from SAA needed for AFA are provided by AM. AFA can also use this service to transfer experimental results to QFA's Visualizer for visualization. On the other hand, SAA can obtain assets from EAMS through the service "EAMS", and these assets can also be transferred to AM and AFA through the corresponding services. It should be noted that only users with the same account number in this architecture and EAMS can share assets between EAMS and SAA. BSFA uses "BSFA-SAA","BSFA-QFA" and "BSFA-AFA" services to provide system services and resource management capabilities to the other three areas.

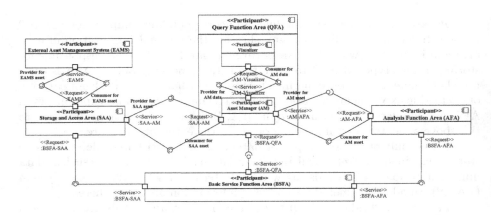

Fig. 2. Software architecture diagram shows the internal composition of each area and interaction with other areas through interfaces.

3   Formal Description of Architecture

The description of existing software architecture design is usually non-formal. In order to have a deeper understanding of architecture, this chapter formalizes the proposed architecture design from the perspective of role.

3.1   Asset

In the discussion of the architecture design, we will refer to scientific data, algorithm and external system collectively as assets and define them in the form of triples.

Definition 1. *Asset*

$$A = (data, algorithm, system) \tag{1}$$

3.2 Component

The concept of a component is defined on top of asset. Component is the basic unit of the architecture, the system developers usually don't need to understand the internal structure of the component, but only focus on the interaction between components. Through components, the architecture can be divided into multiple interactive subsystems, which enhance the independence, scalability and decoupling of the system.

Definition 2. *Component*

$$C = (A_1, \cdots, A_n, S(A_i)) \tag{2}$$

where $i \in [1, n]$, and $S(A_i)$ represents the structures or combinations of assets.

3.3 Interface

The interaction between components is achieved through interface that define the input and output rules of the component and treat the component as a blank box, so that users don't have to care about internal structure of the component.

Definition 3. *Interface*

$$I_{c_p, c_q} = (c_p, c_q), c_q, c_q \in C \tag{3}$$

where c_p represents the request input component, c_q represents the object component.

3.4 Role

For the four areas in the architecture described above, each area contains several components that are functionally similar or grouped together to accomplish a business logic, and the components within the area can interact with each other. The interface of a component which is open to outside is called the interface of that area. This chapter abstracts these areas into four roles, as shown in Table 1.

Definition 4. *Role*

$$R = (c_1, \cdots, c_n, S(c_j), i_{in}, i_{out}), j \in [1, n] \tag{4}$$

where i_{in} are the interfaces between components within the area, i_{out} are the interfaces for area interaction outside, also known as the interfaces for that role.

Table 1. Correspondence of areas and roles

Area	Role	Function
SAA, QFA	Asset owner	Uploading and managing assets
AFA, QFA	Scientist	Conducting scientific experiments
BSFA	System operators	Providing system basic services
ALL	System development	Providing development services

3.5   Architecture

Following the design of the architecture in Sect. 2 and the correspondence of areas and roles, the architecture's formal description is as follows.

Definition 5. *Asset Owner*

$$R(AssetOwner) = (c_R, c_{NR}, c_F, S(c_R, c_{NR}, c_F), i_{in}, i_{out}) \tag{5}$$

where c_R, c_{NR}, c_F represent relational databases, non-relational databases and file systems, which cover most forms of SBD, and

$$i_{out} = (Request : EAMS, Service : SAA - AM, Request : BSFA - SAA) \tag{6}$$

represents externally displayed interfaces.

Definition 6. *Scientist*

$$R(Scientist) = (C_s, S(C_s), i_{in}, i_{out}) \tag{7}$$

where

$$i_{out} = (Request : AM - AFA, Request : BSFA - AFA) \tag{8}$$

contains all requested services of AFA.

Definition 7. *System Operator*

$$R(SystemOperator) = (c_{BS}, c_{RM}, S(c_{BS}, c_{RM}), i_{in}, i_{out}) \tag{9}$$

where c_{BS}, c_{RM} are the related components of system basic services and resource management, and

$$i_{out} = (Service : (BSFA - SAA, BSFA - QFA, BSFA - AFA)) \tag{10}$$

represents its externally displayed interfaces.

Definition 8. *System Developer*

$$R(SystemDeveloper) = (R(AssetOwner, Scientist, SystemOperator)) \tag{11}$$

it shows that the System Developer is a union of three other roles.

Figure 3 shows the interaction between the various roles in this architecture: asset owners are responsible for providing data, algorithms, and other assets in various fields, then assets can be scientifically experimented by scientists and saved in the databases owned by the asset owners; the system operators are responsible for providing resource management functions, monitoring and security measures during this process; the above behaviours are implemented by system developers using a series of tools, and they could perform activities of the other three roles.

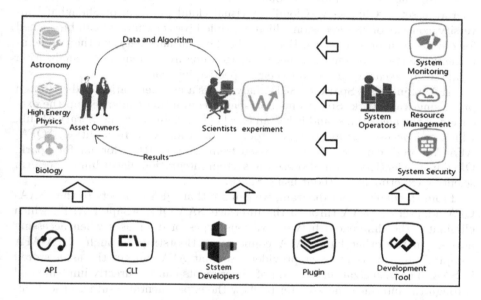

Fig. 3. Assets and information exchange are achieved through communication among various roles. This interactive form promotes the operation of the system.

4   Deployment Architecture as an Implementation of Design

This section describes the integration architecture for the previously defined architecture. The UML deployment diagram is shown in Fig. 4, which presents the main components and communication channels between four areas, along with elements that are used to facilitate communication between these areas.

SAA consists of three different types of databases and one file management system, all run in Linux OS: Mysql as a storage of structured data, MongoDB as a storage of unstructured data, gStore as a storage of RDF graph data and HDFS as a distributed file system. These four components cover almost all kinds of SBD. Since different types of data are stored in different databases or file systems, an adapter named "SAA-QFA Adapter" is required to aggregate the data so that only one unified access interface is displayed externally, reducing the inconsistency caused by accessing different types of data.

SAA is also responsible for connecting with EAMS, in this architecture, EAMS is defined as a material machine learning platform, which uses machine learning methods to analysis material data. The platform is also connected to the SAA-QFA Adapter through an interface, so that the assets of EAMS are consistent with assets in SAA.

Similarly, QFA also consists of two subsystems: Bootstrap as AM, and "Chinese VisCloud" as Visualizer. Bootstrap use a series tools in its framework to operate assets; "Chinese VisCloud", a visual cloud platform of Shanghai University, consists of 48 screens on which multiple browser windows can be opened for cross-screen presentations. Because the data formats between the two components are not consistent, it is necessary to configure an adapter "Visualization Adapter" to exchange data over their respective interfaces.

AFA mainly uses Spark for SBD analysis. As a new generation of distributed processing framework, Spark's memory-based computing can speed up the execution of the algorithms, and it has an excellent machine learning library MLlib, which can be used as an auxiliary tool for data analysis. In addition, "QFA-AFA Adapter" can convert data passed from QFA to RDD format for Spark. Of course, scientists could also use the system integration algorithm to perform scientific experiments without using Spark.

From the deployment diagram, we can see that QFA connects to the "SAA-QFA adapter" in SAA through the interface "SAA-QFA Adapter API", which eliminates the differences between various types of databases when accessing assets. On the other hand, AFA connects to Bootstrap through "QFA-AFA Adapter" and interface "asset provider", so that AFA can get the asset stored in SAA. The visualization function of experiments can be directly implemented through the interface and adapter to show the experimental results to the "Chinese VisCloud" or Bootstrap.

Besides the above three areas, BSFA consists of three components: a Java security framework, Apache Shiro, which provides security features such as identity privilege verification and single sign-on for the architecture; a common resource management system, Apache YARN, which can provide unified resource management and scheduling for upper-layer applications, its introduction brings huge benefits to clusters in terms of utilization, unified resource management, and data sharing; a web-based tool, Apache Ambari, which supports cluster provisioning, management, and monitoring. These functions and services are supported through the "BSFA Adapter" and "Basic service provider" for other areas.

5   Architecture Application Scenario

This section will demonstrate and illustrate the typical application scenario of the above architecture under different roles.

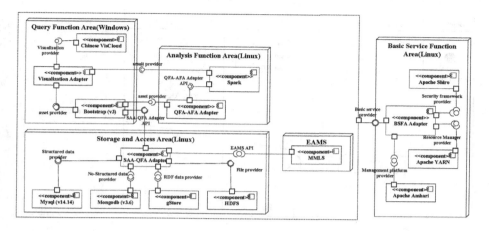

Fig. 4. The UML deployment diagram presents the main components, communication channels and technological requirements of four areas.

5.1   Conducting Scientific Experiments by Scientists

The main goal of scientists conducting scientific experiments is to make a good decision by constantly changing the combination of data and algorithms and observing the experimental results. Scientists often run different script files on the local machine to combine data and algorithms to form different scientific experiments. They may also be necessary to obtain corresponding data from different databases, and it will make the preparation of scientific experiments very tedious. The architecture integrates various types of data and algorithms in different fields. From the scientists' point of view, these assets are the same, and there is no difference due to storage in different databases. At the same time, the scientists only need to select the data and algorithms, and fill in the necessary parameters. It is not necessary to modify and debug the script as before, which greatly enhances the efficiency and user experience of scientists in conducting scientific experiments.

Scientists' process of conducting scientific experiments in the architecture is as follows: first of all, scientists should register the experimental information, including experiment name, type, number of steps, running environment, and so on; afterwards, scientists could freely select the required data and algorithms on the page, no matter what domains of these assets, and no matter whether stored in a relational or non-relational database, scientists just need to click the select and search box; finally, the experiment is started by clicking the "Start Analysis" button; the results of the experiment will be displayed on the page, scientists can choose to view and save it. Figure 5 shows scientists' activity model and the steps that AFA take in the above process.

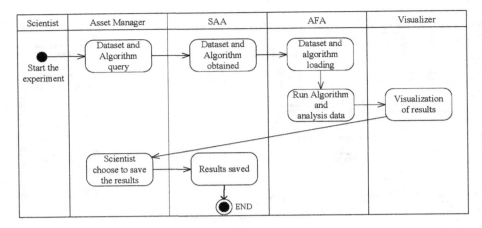

Fig. 5. Scientists' activity model related to conducting scientific experiments, and the steps that each area takes in the model.

5.2   Data Quality Detection by Asset Owner

Data is the carrier of information, and the quality of data is of great significance to correctly reflect the scientific significance of it and to effectively support decision-making. On the basis of the above research, this paper adopts the following data quality detection methods for scientific data: field incompleteness detection, numerical field detection and data set sampling survey.

The first on is field incomplete detection. The incompleteness of a field is divided into two cases: unassigned and undefined. Unassigned corresponding field content is empty, and undefined indicates that the field value is unknown (NULL). In fact, an empty field is a valid character, and NULL is a special kind of value, unlike a zero-length string. In this architecture, the above two cases are treated as incomplete fields.

The second one is numeric field detection. Because most of the scientific data are numerical, a series of statistical methods are used to check whether the data are within a reasonable range and the distribution of the data, etc. These methods include average, inter-quartile, standard deviation, skewness, and upper and low limit method.

The last one is data set sampling survey. A sample survey takes a small number of samples, conducts an actual investigation of them, and verifies the authenticity of the data. Sampling includes simple random sampling, stratified random sampling, cluster sampling, system sampling, etc. Considering the differences between SBD, simple random sampling is chosen as the sampling method.

5.3   Providing System Services by System Operators

While the system operators are responsible for system basic services and resource management functions, they can view various information during the current system runtime, such as system environment variable information, system configuration attributes, operating system information, and file system information. The system performance information, like CPU utilization (user utilization, system utilization, and total utilization), memory and swap usage, and network situation can also be observed. Through the above information, the system operators could clearly understand the operation of the current system, and could timely capture the abnormal information for processing.

5.4   Super Administrator for System Developers

In this architecture, the system developers are similar to a super administrator and have all rights of scientists, asset owners, and system operators. They have all functions and can perform user management, rights configuration, and other activities.

6   Conclusion

This paper proposes a software architecture model to manage multi-domain and heterogeneous SBD. Asset storage, analysis, visualization, and external systems access are integrated into one architecture through different services which are implemented by RESTFul interfaces. In addition, this paper formalizes the design of the architecture from the perspective of role to have a deeper understanding of the architecture in the future.

The highlights of the proposed architecture are: (1) Integration of multiple types of databases and provision of external system access capabilities to manage and share multi-source heterogeneous scientific data; (2) the role division of the architecture is proposed to describe the formal definition of each element in the architecture design; (3) this paper shows the architecture's typical application scenarios form the perspective of role, and solves the problems of management and utilization of SBD to some extent.

In future research, we will use formal, systematic, and standardized evaluation methods to evaluate the proposed architecture. The process of scientific experiment will be focused to further design and improve the four areas. In addition, based on the evolution of SBD, the origin and development of data will be further reflected in the architecture.

Acknowledgement. This work is supported by the National Key Research and Development Plan of China (Grant No. 2016YFB1000600 and 2016YFB1000601).

References

1. Andreeva, J., Campana, S., Fanzago, F., Herrala, J.: High-energy physics on the grid: the atlas and CMS experience. J. Grid Comput. **6**(1), 3–13 (2008)
2. Bengtssonpalme, J., et al.: Strategies to improve usability and preserve accuracy in biological sequence databases. Proteomics **16**(18), 2454–2460 (2016)
3. Cook, C.E., Bergman, M.T., Cochrane, G., Apweiler, R., Birney, E.: The European bioinformatics institute in 2017: data coordination and integration. Nucleic Acids Res. **46**(D1), D21 (2018)
4. Dewitt, D.J., Kabra, N., Luo, J., Patel, J.M., Yu, J.B.: Client–server paradise. In: Proceedings of the 20th International Conference on Very Large Data Bases, pp. 558–569 (1994)
5. Dozier, J., Stonebraker, M., Frew, J.: Sequoia 2000: a next-generation information system for the study of global change. In: Proceedings Thirteenth IEEE Symposium on Mass Storage Systems. Towards Distributed Storage and Data Management Systems, pp. 47–53 (1994)
6. Gao, W., et al.: Data motif-based proxy benchmarks for big data and AI workloads. In: IISWC 2018 (2018)
7. Gao, W., et al.: Data motifs: a lens towards fully understanding big data and AI workloads. In: 27th International Conference on Parallel Architectures and Compilation Techniques, PACT 2018 (2018)
8. Ivanova, M., Nes, N., Goncalves, R., Kersten, M.: MonetDB/SQL meets skyserver: the challenges of a scientific database. In: International Conference on Scientific and Statistical Database Management, p. 13 (2007)
9. Ivezic, Z., et al.: LSST: from science drivers to reference design and anticipated data products. Am. Astron. Soc. **41**, 366 (2008)
10. Jia, Z., et al.: Understanding big data analytics workloads on modern processors. IEEE Trans. Parallel Distrib. Syst. **28**(6), 1797–1810 (2017)
11. Jun, C., Wen, W., Zi-yang, L., An, L.: Landsat 5 satellite overview. Remote Sens. Inf. **43**(3), 85–89 (2007)
12. Stonebraker, M.: Scientific data bases at scale and SciDB. Anal. Proc. **4**, 199–206 (2013)
13. Suchanek, F.M., Weikum, G.: Knowledge bases in the age of big data analytics. VLDB Endowment (2014)
14. Szalay, A.S., Gray, J., Fekete, G., Kunszt, P.Z., Kukol, P., Thakar, A.: Indexing the sphere with the hierarchical triangular mesh. Microsoft Research (2007)
15. Team, C.T.P.: Paradise: a database system for gis applications. In: ACM SIGMOD International Conference on Management of Data, p. 485 (1995)
16. Wang, L., et al.: Bigdatabench: a big data benchmark suite from internet services. In: IEEE International Symposium on High Performance Computer Architecture, HPCA 2014 (2014)

Author Index

Printed in the United States
By Bookmasters